TRANSFORMING
AUSTIN
- A GOD STORY

BY THANA ROLPH

THANKS

I want to thank all of the men and women who have shared their stories with me, and I want to apologize that I couldn't use all of them. I have learned so much from you. A special thanks goes to Barbara Bucklin, who generously shared her decades of research into Austin's history as well as her knowledge of those who have played key roles in the past quarter century, and to June Criner, for the hours she spent in the libraries digging out the spiritual history, so she could pray over it.

Thanks to Ashton and Jennifer Cumberbatch, who opened the door to the African-American community for me. A special thanks to Dan Davis, who handed me his manuscript and told me to use anything I wanted, and, more importantly, for the half century of his life he's poured into knowing, loving, and unifying the pastors of this city. A great big thank you to Alan Nagel, who encouraged me to write this book and who has enabled me to understand major principles of city transformation.

Finally, thanks to my daughter, Cheri Mayott, who spent many hours editing this manuscript, and to my grandson, Matt Gore, whose beautiful photograph graces the cover.

ENDORSEMENT

Watching God's Spirit operate in the lives of individuals throughout a city is very fulfilling and speaks loudly of the prayers of many believers. This book shares story after story of "God Showing up" in Austin! Some examples of what God has done include: unity among pastors, a growing number of intercessors, a greater openness toward spiritual things among non-believers, believers beginning to "live on mission," and many others.

My prayer for this book is that it would encourage believers in other communities to love their city with Christ's love in such a way that every man, woman, and child will see, hear, and come to understand that Christ loves them.

Alan Nagel
Former Executive Director of ABBA
CRU City Coach
Austin, Texas

TABLE OF CONTENTS

FOREWORD

G od is at work in our cities. We hear many reports that Christ
is transforming his church and, through it, transforming
the cities of our nation and of the world. Churches are increas-
ingly taking responsibility for the lostness of their cities. They are
proclaiming and living out a broad-based Gospel of redemption
and reconciliation. We celebrate that He has not bypassed Austin,
and we rejoice in how we see the transformation that has been
launched here.

Austin is a bit of an anomaly in the state of Texas. It is gir-
dled by a conservative belt of cities like Dallas, Fort Worth,
Houston, and Lubbock. It is the blue island in the red sea of the
state. Culturally, Austin is much more akin to San Francisco and
Portland. I have observed the spiritual life of Austin for the past
thirty years. In those early years, the church was marginalized in
the cultural life of the city. However, I have seen an acceleration
of positive attitudes regarding Christ's work, including the work
of the church in our city. This is God's doing!

In this book, Thana Rolph has researched and reported this
transformation in Austin and the central Texas region. She has
provided both a historical and a cultural context for the church
in this time of transition. She reports on a church IN the city that
is FOR the city, no longer isolated, but developing influence for
living the Gospel beyond the walls of our homes and churches.

In reports of this type, we are often tempted to focus on
our own contribution as being the key to the changes that have

happened. Thana has resisted this temptation, reporting on the broad stream of Christ's work.

I believe that this work will complement those from other cities in chronicling what God is doing in our time.

Daniel Davis

Pastor Emeritus of Hope Chapel-Austin

Co-Founder of Austin Bridge Builders Alliance (ABBA)

Austin, Texas

INTRODUCTION

I was enjoying a springtime scene from a ski slope in Colorado, filled with gratitude for the beauty, which enveloped me in the sweet presence of God. The sense of His presence became almost tangible as I sensed Him asking me, "Do you want to write My story?"

The question caught me totally off guard. I didn't know what to do with it. "Your story was written a long time ago," I replied, but what I was really saying was, "What on earth are You talking about?" Over the next few weeks I came to understand that God's story has no end. He is living and moving through His kids all over the planet all the time. In reality, your story is God's story, written in the unfolding pages of your life. My specific assignment seemed to be the story of what God had been doing and is doing in and around Austin—the Central Texas story. Even that was much too large to comprehend.

The Lord had strategically placed me at Austin Bridge Builders Alliance (ABBA), which is a connecting and convening organization, seeking the principles and practical applications for transforming a city. I began interviewing many people who had been instrumental in the changes of the last forty years and reading the materials they pointed me to about those who had gone before. While I regret that there are doubtless many important events I have not captured and many significant people I have not mentioned, I hope you will see, as I have, that this truly is God's story.

There are two major themes to which I have tried to be faithful. The first is to choose the people and events that have been bridges to bring the Body of Christ together to become a significant force for the Kingdom of God in the area. Some were forerunners, some builders, and some connectors. They have all contributed to the flow of events that have changed and are changing the heart of Central Texas.

The other theme is harder to define. It has to do with the importance of a brand of unity that respects and grows out of diversity. In the midst of my interviews, I watched a movie about the nation's founding fathers. I was impressed with the contrast between John Adams and Thomas Jefferson. They each had a piece that was essential to forming our nation. Each also carried a philosophy that, without balance, could have destroyed this country. Jefferson's piece, democracy in which every man has a say, carried to the extreme, would have produced anarchy. Adams' insistence on centralized government, unchecked, could have led back to monarchy. God put them together to form a nation with the strongest voice for freedom the world has known. No one man could have founded this nation. It took many men and women, passionate about very different things, who under God's hand, melded their strengths and countered their weaknesses to found a structure that other men and women could build on.

As the Lord orchestrates a unified thrust toward transforming our city or any city, it takes all our strengths and all our passions to overcome all our weaknesses and truly represent Jesus as Lord in the city. My heart is that the Lord would use the amazing stories and wise insight, from the widely diverse people represented here, to help each reader discover a broader, richer picture of Jesus and to appreciate the many facets of His character portrayed through His people.

Chapter 1

What Starts Here . . .

We step into a place in time that is neither the beginning nor the end of a thing. God has already been there, already been working, already been forming something, already been preparing the good works that we are to walk in. We occupy the time and the season prepared for us and thus fulfill our destiny.

In the heart of Austin sits the University of Texas, whose motto states, "What starts here changes the world." While our story starts long before there was a university, that theme seems to have already existed in the heart of God.

In 1820 no citizen of the United States was allowed on Texas soil without a passport from the Spanish Viceroy. One man, only one man, Moses Austin . . .

"Not deterred by the race hatred engendered by years of invasion . . . presented himself before Martinez, the governor of the province, in San Antonio . . . . The fact that he had come without a passport from the Spanish viceroy provoked the anger of Martinez, and he ordered Austin to depart from Texas.

> When he (Austin) left the office of Martinez and was crossing the old civil plaza in San Antonio, sick and disappointed, he met the Baron de Bastrop, whom he had known in Louisiana. Bastrop took him to his home, nursed him through sickness, reconciled Martinez and obtained from him permission to colonize three hundred families. That casual meeting with the Baron de Bastrop changed the map of North America . . . ."[1]

What drove Moses Austin to such extremes? He had a dream. His vision was of a city called Austina, which would be the crossroads for an Empire, with great commerce and trade, a city of grandeur and magnificence to rival New Orleans, with wide thoroughfares, the seat of government, and with a university as its heart and backbone. He believed it would influence the world.[2] He believed it so strongly that he gave what was left of his life and made his son, Stephen F. Austin, promise to dedicate his life to the fulfillment of the vision.

The premise of this book is that long before there was a University of Texas or a Moses Austin, the Lord already had plans for Central Texas. Both Moses and Stephen Austin laid hold of their part of God's vision. So did many others, some of whose stories are recorded here. The point is not to exalt a place in Texas. The point is to look for what God has done and is doing in this city and in your city through ordinary folks like you and me. It's to explore, not so much patterns, but principles that seem to be relevant in bringing change to a city. It's to look at the dreams and purposes God has planted in your own heart and consider how to lay hold of them and see where they fit in the greater scheme of things. It's about God's heart for renewal.

So was Moses Austin's "casual meeting" with Baron de Bastrop a coincidence, or was it another step in the eternal plan of God? Read on and judge for yourself, and as you read, take time to look at what God has been doing and is doing in the place where you live.

END NOTES

1. From the speech by the Hon. A. W. Terrell on January 17, 1889; Proceedings in the House of Representatives, Twenty-first Legislature of the Presentation to Texas of a Full Length Portrait of Stephen F. Austin—reproduced from holdings of the Texas State Archives

2. From a speech called "History of Austin," by Barbara Bucklin on November 2005 at an ABBA event for new pastors.

Chapter 2

GATHERING LIVING STONES

The Apostle Peter once called the early church, which by then had been spread over a broad area of the known world, "living stones" forming a "spiritual house" of which Jesus was the chief cornerstone (1 Peter 2:5). Over the centuries, those living stones have shaped themselves together to reflect Jesus' ministry in various ways. Some express His holiness, some His compassion, and others His power. Some work tirelessly to share the good news of salvation, and others to bring justice to the downtrodden. So what face of Jesus came to Texas? They all did—in their own way and in the Lord's timing.

Because the Spanish were the first to lay claim to Texas, the first Christian influence was Roman Catholic. In 1730 the Spanish had set up a mission near what is now Barton Springs, but it was soon moved to San Antonio. When Stephen F. Austin began registering men for land grants in Central Texas, the Mexican government offered generous land grants with the stipulation that the recipients become Mexican citizens and convert to the Catholic faith. In addition, they had to be men of good morals and proven character.

While Catholicism was the official religion, there were very few priests in all of Texas. In 1834, Mary Austin Holley, Stephen F. Austin's sister, said of the territory of Texas: "Texas was not, like New England, settled by Puritans flying from persecution. It was, however, settled by men who knew the value of freedom of conscience as well as of civil liberty. They accepted lands from the Mexican government on condition of becoming nominal Catholics . . . They knew that for them the best creed was a familiar one— general enough surely to offend no one— *'Be good and mind your work.'* . . . Hence, all have been silent on the subject of religion, and there is not to this day a church in the colonies. Some have objected to Texas—*it is no place for them*—*there is no religion there.* With their Bibles in their hands, can they not carry their religion in their hearts, and act it out in their lives, where there are none to molest or make them afraid?"[1]

Independence opened the door for other people of faith

As soon as Texas won its independence from Mexico in 1836, Protestant missionaries and circuit riders began to trickle into the territory. The first church service held in Austin was on October 13, 1839, at Bullock's Hotel, called by a Presbyterian minister, the Reverend William Y. Allen. That was two and one-half months before the city of Austin was chartered, on December 27, 1839. The would-be congregation was dispersed by fear of Indian raids, which caused many citizens to flee to Washington on the Brazos.[2]

Native Americans proved to be an issue in the area for several years. In 1839 the Reverend John Haynie, the first Methodist circuit rider to brave the area, riding from Bastrop to the soon-to-be Travis County, refused to carry a gun, but his successor, the Rev. Josiah Whipple, kept a rifle and a pistol in the pulpit.[3]

The Methodists held services in a log house in 1840, then built the first church building in the area in 1847. They are also credited with establishing the first Sunday school in Austin. In 1848, when Dr. Daniel Baker was sent by the Presbyterian Church to hold evangelistic services in Austin, he found what he called, "an admirably conducted Sabbath school."[4]

With the admission of Texas into the United States in 1845, Baptists entered the state with a missionary conquest. In his address at the Diamond Jubilee of the Austin Baptist Association in 1932, J. N. Marshall described the pioneer missionary of the early days of Austin Baptists:

> The frontier missionary went on horseback with a pair of saddlebags strapped across the cantle of his saddle, with a Bible in one bag and hymn book in the other and the sparsest amount of change in clothing. He says his tearful good-byes to loved ones, and starts his months' journeys ... He preached in private homes and little school houses, and when he finds a little encouragement, and the spirit seems to be moving among the people, he tarries for a few days' meetings.[5]

It was not only the ministers on horseback that carried the message of Christ. Baptist pastors and their congregations showed a burning passion for spreading the gospel among lost people. The growth of the Baptist work across the years is due largely to the enduring emphasis put on evangelism.

Another strength the Baptists have consistently brought to the table is their adherence to the Bible. They have contributed much to Christian education, from the pulpit and in the classroom. The scriptural seed planted by the Baptists has produced a variety of fruit. Many current leaders of evangelical and charismatic churches received their grounding in the Word of God under Baptist instruction.

The Civil War broke up congregations

Austin's fledgling congregations hit a hard bump in the road as the nation edged into the conflict that became the Civil War. An Episcopal congregation, then called The Church of the Epiphany, erected a building downtown in 1853-54. "In 1856 about twenty members with Northern sympathies withdrew and called the Reverend Charles Gillette to organize a new parish named Christ Church. The new church held its services in the courtroom of the new county courthouse. In 1859 Edward Fontaine resigned as Rector of The Church of the Epiphany and moved to Jackson,

Mississippi. At that point there existed two parishes: one with a rector but no church building, and one with a building and no rector."[6] When the two groups reconciled, they renamed the body St. David's.

While the St. David's story is depictive of the struggle that went on in many of the area congregations, it is more than that. St. David's main building is one of the oldest remaining structures in downtown Austin. It has seen division, undergone remodeling, and faced extinction, but it still stands, symbolic of the larger, "capital C Church" in the city, which stands solid at the core, planted in the heart of God, regardless of division, remodeling, and structurally weak elements in need of repair.

Seeds of compassion and justice

In the wake of the Civil War, several Christian "streams" cooperated to try to right some of the effects of slavery. The American Missionary Association (AMA), made up mostly of Methodists, Congregationalists, and Presbyterians from both white and black races, worked to establish schools and colleges for freed slaves. Tillotson Collegiate and Normal Institute was chartered as a coeducational school in 1877 and opened January 17, 1881. Samuel Huston College, birthed out of the Methodist Episcopal conference with the help of the Freedman's Aid Society, backed by the AMA, opened in 1900. The two schools merged in 1952 becoming Huston-Tillotson College.[7]

The Lord's compassion has also flowed through the Catholic Church in several practical ways.[8] One was health care. In 1897, a group of Austin women known as the St. Vincent's Aid Society, distressed over the city hospital's disregard for religious matters, invited the Daughters of Charity of St. Vincent de Paul to come to Austin to operate a new hospital.[9] In 1902 Seton Infirmary was dedicated, containing seventeen private rooms and eleven wards. In 1936 the Reverend Francis R. Weber established Holy Cross Catholic Church in East Austin. Known as "the Carpenter Priest," Reverend Weber soon built a Catholic school at 1106 Concho, but while in the process, he discovered a much greater need. He discovered there was no affordable medical care for the black community, so he converted the building to a hospital. The Holy Cross Hospital gave quality medical care for fifty years.[10]

A new dimension of the Holy Spirit

The expression of Jesus that demonstrated the gifts and power of the Holy Spirit was revived in the United States in Topeka, Kansas, right at the turn of the twentieth century. That tiny movement was fanned in a worldwide flame at Azusa Street in Los Angeles. Those meetings started April 14, 1906, but even before Azusa Street, the fire was already burning in Central Texas. Barbara Dugone and Jo Leslie, daughters of Larry Donahue, who founded Glad Tidings Assembly of God Church in Austin, told of their family's history, so deeply entwined in the story of Central Texas. Their mother was the great-granddaughter of John Henry Lohmann, for whom Lohmans Crossing was named. Fred Lohmann, grandson of John Henry, received the baptism of the Holy Spirit in 1902, along with his two sisters (one of which was Barbara and Jo's grandmother) and a brother-in-law, Les Jones. Fred and Les of the holiness movement became itinerate preachers and preached throughout the area. They were also among the founders of the Assemblies of God Church, which was founded in Hot Springs, Arkansas, in 1914.

One of the places they preached was in a small church called Loafer's Glory, just north of Liberty Hill. The name was coined because of the kindness of local residents to transients. Word spread that the area was a great place to get a hot meal and a warm bed. Meetings started, and a small church was established. "In 1902 residents invited George Sutton, grandfather of evangelist Hilton Sutton, to conduct revival services. The services started early and went long into the night as people from all over central Texas gathered to sing hymns and hear preaching in a small revival tent."[11] Fred Lohmann pastored the Loafer's Glory Apostolic Church for a season. For almost twenty years the church continued to grow and witness miraculous healings until the Great Depression forced the residents to seek a living elsewhere. The White Stone Assemblies of God Church in Cedar Park was birthed out of that revival movement.

So parts of the Body of Christ came to Central Texas. They represented every color and creed, and for the most part they weren't connected at all. They were more like separate little piles of stones that God was gathering. They weren't ready to become a united "spiritual house." Each group did its own thing, but among them God was worshipped, His word went forth, people received Jesus, justice and compassion had a voice, righteousness took small stands, and the gifts and power of the Holy Spirit were seeded into the area. Central Texas was a hard place; the beginnings were small, but God gathered His precious stones to begin to clear the way for those who would build on those beginnings.

Questions to consider:
1. Do a little research on the history of the Christian influence in your city.
   What's there?
   Why is it there?

2. Prayerfully consider what each part contributed. How did God use their movements? What would the city be lacking if that piece were missing?

3. What insight have you discovered about The Body of Christ?

END NOTES
1. Mary Austin Holley, *Texas: Original Narratives of Texas History and Adventure*, (Austin: The Steck Company, 1935), 176–177.
2. "Expanded History, The Organization of the First Presbyterian Church," accessed September 7, 2012. http://www.fpcaustin.org/history/article296566.htm?links=1&body=1.

3. "History of First Church," First United Methodist Church of Austin, Texas, accessed September 7, 2012, http://fumcaustin.org/about-us/history/.
4. "Expanded History, The Organization of the First Presbyterian Church," accessed September 7, 2012.
5. James M. Sapp revised by David W. Smith, *A Persistent People*, (Austin Baptist Association, Austin, TX, 2008), 10–11.
6. "St. David's Episcopal Church: History," accessed September 7, 2012.http://stdave.org/site/about/cat/history/.
7. "Huston-Tillotson University," accessed September 7, 2012. http://en.wikipedia.org/wiki/Huston–Tillotson_University.
8. In 1841, Bishop Jean Marie Odin traveled to Austin and successfully argued with government officials for the reclamation of Catholic Church property, which had been confiscated by the Republic of Texas. The first Catholic Church, built in the 1850's was called St. Patrick's but was renamed St. Mary's and was upgraded to a cathedral. From the "Catholic Archives of Texas."
9. "Seton Healthcare Family–Central Texas History and Heritage – About Seton," accessed August 21, 2012, http://www.seton.net/about_seton/setons_history_and_heritage/central_texas.
10. Holy Cross Catholic Church 75th Anniversary book.
11. Dickinson, Louis Don. "Loafer's Glory." *The Good News Journal*, October 1997.

Chapter 3

OUTSIDE THE STAINED GLASS WINDOWS

In 1969, when Evelyn Davison, now National Day of Prayer leader for Central Texas, moved to Austin with her husband, Van, she didn't believe God lived here. In Cut and Shoot, Texas, where she grew up, everyone turned out when someone needed help regardless of what church they attended. In Austin, Evelyn couldn't find the Christian community outside the walls of the church. She recalled, "One of the first things that I remember bringing people out from behind the stained glass windows and leveling the ground for denominations was Christian Women's Club, which was an offshoot of Stonecroft Ministries, based in Kansas City, Missouri. In 1970 they started with a women's club where we who were Christians would invite unbelievers to come to lunch. Out of that came Friendship Bible Coffees and women's prayer groups in the neighborhoods. We'd put up a sign saying, 'Women praying here.'" Evelyn thought those were the first chinks in the walls that separated the denominational people from one another.[1]

Here's Life, Austin

Some of those women helped form a prayer nucleus for a citywide campaign called "Here's Life, Austin." Campus Crusade had chosen Atlanta to try out a pilot program for "Here's Life, America," meant to saturate cities with the Gospel. In 1974, Crusade sent Alan Nagel to develop the plan in Austin. Alan spent the first year getting to know pastors in Central Texas and the second, helping churches organize training for a month long event called the "I Found It" campaign, which took place in 1976. Alan described the campaign like this:

> There were eighty churches participating. Each one committed to cover a geographic area, usually a zip code. They did a ton of training all over the city. They trained people how to share their faith in Christ. The first week of the actual campaign, all they did was put the phrase "I found it" up all over town—on bumper stickers, pins, billboards, etc. That's all it said, no detail. Then everybody was starting to ask the question, "What did you find?" The next week all of the billboards, all the ads changed. They said, "I found it—new life in Christ. Call 458-2111." For the next two weeks the blitz was on. There was a phone bank set up to take the calls. They advertised in the newspaper, on billboards all over the city, and on-spot announcements on television networks. A commercial spot would come on with a variety of people saying they found it and where to call, and the phone bank would light up. Next to it they had a war room where all eighty churches were listed with their zip codes, so when someone called, a card with their info would go into the box of the church that was handling that zip code. Once a day the church got the cards. Trained people would take the cards and a little booklet called 'I Found It.' The book contained testimonies of recognizable people telling how they found Christ, and it had the four spiritual laws in the back. So a trained person would deliver the booklet and take it from there.

★ 26 ★

This campaign was significant on various levels. Probably the most obvious is that eighty churches, which were not accustomed to looking much beyond the walls of their own buildings, learned they could work together for the good of the city—at least for one event. Pastors got to know each other and began to form relationships. Many lay people were trained to share their faith. Parachurch groups, designed to minister in adult communities like the military and the business community, built lasting structures.

Another powerful thing that came out of "Here's Life, Austin" was an introduction to the Great Commission Prayer Crusade, which was headed up by Vonette Bright, wife of Campus Crusade leader, Bill Bright. In Austin, Vonette found Frances Bradley and asked her to head up the Great Commission Prayer Crusade for Austin. It became the prayer arm of the "Here's Life" campaign. Several churches committed to pray for the campaign—some continued praying 24/7 even after the campaign ended. Frances said the Hyde Park Baptist Church continued to pray around the clock for several years.

A less obvious plan of God has taken longer to unfold. God works through individuals, sometimes going to great lengths to train them for places and positions that cannot be seen apart from the unfolding of time. Alan Nagel worked hard to build relationships in Austin. After heading up "Here's Life, America," which eventually touched 253 metropolitan areas,[1] he became part of a leadership team developing adult ministry globally. The next twenty-five years he provided leadership in team building and in uniting that which defies union in God's school of life. He had no way of knowing he would go full circle and bring every tool he gained on that journey back to Austin for a different level of city transformation. We'll catch that story in a later chapter.

The Well—an ecumenical miracle

Meanwhile, back in the sixties, several movements were crisscrossing the nation. The Ecumenical Movement, the Charismatic Movement, and the Jesus People phenomenon were all working to tear down the denominational walls that kept the Body of Christ fractured. In Austin in 1964, Nancy Pickens, a Presbyterian, was attending a Bible study at Saint David's Episcopal Church. The St. David's pastor, Charles Sumners, prayed a simple prayer for a friend of Nancy's, who had been fighting a staph infection for weeks, and she was instantly healed. That reality of God's presence and personal involvement started Dick and Nancy Pickens on a journey that touched on a lot of what God was doing in the nation at that time. While remaining in the Presbyterian Church, they became involved in the Charismatic movement, were touched by Full Gospel Businessmen, and found themselves drawing together what had always been separate. After being ordained by the Austin Presbyterian Theological Seminary, Dick worked with Teen Challenge, under the auspices of the Assemblies of God, to help start an off-campus ministry called The Well.

The Well was a real breakthrough ministry in Austin. Located in an old fraternity house at the corner of 26th and Nueces, The Well was staffed by a diverse group, which included a Catholic priest and a variety of Protestants, all with the aim of showing God's love to anyone who needed it. They were one of the first groups to minister to the homeless. The house was open 24/7 to help people high on drugs or down on life. They had live Christian music at their coffeehouse on Fridays and Saturdays and a time of worship and teaching on Sundays, which didn't conflict with worship in the local churches. So far, as we can tell, they were the first live worship music venue in Austin.

Tragedy and life

On August 1, 1966, a student at the University of Texas, Charles Whitman, went on a shooting rampage from the UT Tower, killing seventeen people, including himself, and wounding thirty-two others. Within the next decade, the Lord seemed to say to the devil, "I'll see your tragedy and raise you a royal flush of life." He brought key leaders, like Evelyn Davison and Alan Nagel, to the city, and rose up others from within. Women began to pray in neighborhoods; multitudes learned to share the Gospel; groups started forming across denominational lines to help those in need and to reach out to people in all walks of life; and live worship moved outside the church into the heart of the city. Perhaps these were small beginnings—but throughout the seventies, the Holy Spirit made cracks in the walls that separated parts of His Body, opened doors to new alliances and to new forms of ministry and worship, and began to shift the spiritual climate of the area. Although no one realized what God was doing, that shift, from the lone warrior and isolated congregation toward a unified thrust, had begun. The church of Austin was beginning to move outside the stained glass windows.

Questions to consider:
1. Look at the history of your city. What events, positive and negative, have laid a foundation for where you are today?
2. Who have been the key players in where your city is today?
3. Can you see any relational pattern to events? Ask the Lord to show you the pieces He has been drawing together and fitting into place.

END NOTES
1. Evelyn wasn't aware of the CROP walks that began in East Austin that same year. CROP Hunger Walks are community fund-raising events sponsored by Church World Service to increase awareness and aid for the poor. Various denominational churches joined forces, and the first official CROP Hunger Walk was held in Austin in 1970 and raised $5067–a large amount in those days. http://austincrophungerwalk.org/.
2. http://www.rebuildjournal.org/articles/evanglifstylp-strlrnwl.html.

Chapter 4

"I Will Build My Church"

While The Well was at its height, the young vice president of a small software company was asked to lead a semester Bible study for some University of Texas students. The semester grew into years, and Dan Davis found himself pastor of a small church they called Hope Chapel. Several couples that had been involved in The Well joined the church. Dan recounted, "Those people were significant in making Hope Chapel what it became. They had a forerunner effect on the church." Their stability and strength helped undergird the next major move that God had in store for Austin.

God moved in a number of ways in the city through Dan. From the inception of his church, he recognized the need for building relationship with other pastors. He recalled:

> My biggest concern was that the rest of the body of Christ in the city wouldn't accept us as legitimate. We were not sponsored by a denomination or by any other church or movement. I had not gone to Bible school or seminary . . . just a rag-tag bunch of young people and an ex-businessman and his wife. So I took the initiative of cold calling a different pastor each week, telling him that I was a new

pastor in the city and would like to get acquainted. I was pleasantly surprised that almost all the pastors I called agreed to go to lunch with me. I was further surprised to discover that, while I was calling for the fairly selfish reason of gaining their acceptance, many of them were just as desirous of sharing friendship with me.

That began a pattern that has continued through the years. It was a very important learning experience for me, and I believe, for the other pastors as well. Since these encounters were purely relational, it was easy to get into conversations about our differences in beliefs, unencumbered by an agenda to try to change the other person's stance on various doctrinal matters. The conversations were shaped by the desire to understand rather than to convert. I was surprised to discover the stereotypes that others had about Charismatics in general. I was equally surprised to discover the stereotypes that I had formed of others not in my own stream.[1]

As Dan's view of interrelating in the Body of Christ began to change, so did his perspective of the meaning and purpose of church. In 1984, he attended a Perspectives Course, geared to reshape one's theology to view the Bible as God's great plan for reaching all nations and peoples. *It presents "mission" as the purpose for the church, rather than a department in the church.* Steve Hawthorne, who co-authored the course, was one of the guest speakers. He presented a project for building teams and training them to go into major cities of unreached peoples. He challenged members of the Perspectives Class to consider joining a four-month long project—the first month spent at the U.S. Center for World Missions in Pasadena, California, and the last three months in on-the-ground work in a large city where there was little penetration of the Gospel. Dan volunteered to lead a team to Istanbul, Turkey.

In Istanbul, Dan and his wife, Joann, used principles that Steve had developed while leading prayer teams in Egypt. They learned firsthand the power of prayerwalking as their team walked the streets of Istanbul and watched God open doors and bring contacts. They brought the concept of prayerwalking home to Austin with them.

One church, many expressions

That's not all they brought home from Turkey. They rubbed shoulders with various ministries and movements and gained a much larger perspective of the body of Christ in general and of CHURCH in particular. "Our goal is to seek greater unity in the body of Christ in Austin and the larger central Texas region. In pursuing that goal the use of the term "church" to identify an individual congregation is counter-productive. *Therefore, I suggest that we will limit the use of the term "church" to the one body of Christ in our region and refer to individual expressions as congregations.* 1 Corinthians 12 describes the Body of Christ being composed of many members, each with a specific function or role to play. The primary meaning of this passage applies to the different gifts that individuals exercise in the congregation. I see a broader application wherein the individual congregations represent the members of the church in the city. This helps me to better understand the diversity of congregations that make up the church. A city is too large and diverse for one congregation to be all things to all people . . . All the congregations in the city have unique gifts that should be exercised as their part of the church in the city."

Dan's belief in one church with many expressions has guided much of what he has helped build in the area. You'll learn more about that in other chapters. In the late eighties and early nineties his focus on relationship with other pastors laid a foundation for much of what was to follow. Beyond the get-acquainted lunches, he began meeting to fellowship and pray with four other pastors every Wednesday morning. In 1997, Charles Patterson (Church of the Hills), Dennis Hall (Round Rock Chapel), Rick Randall (Austin

Cornerstone), and Dan went to Phoenix to join an old friend of Dan's, Gary Kinnaman of Mesa, Arizona, to discuss a small group approach to meet the needs of pastors.

> In Phoenix, we discussed the immense value that our small groups in Austin and Phoenix had served in restoring our souls in the midst of ongoing ministry. We had all experienced the safety of being part of a non-hierarchical, committed small group of men who shared and understood the joy, the trauma, the pain, and sometimes the isolation of the pastoral calling. We understood that our bond was relational, not organizational, and that all members of the group were mutually committed to the group. Thus emerged the idea of a covenant bond among the members of a group small enough to provide time for each member to share.

> Returning to Austin, our group began to prayerfully take steps to implement what had been decided in Phoenix. By that time, I had served as a pastor for over twenty years and had many trusted pastor friends. Most of the others in our group had served here for over ten years, and we had met in our group for most of those ten years, so we had a running start promoting the concept to others. All the guys in the group started planning to develop their own new groups.

Pastors in Covenant (PIC) groups now serve well over a hundred area pastors in small groups where deep relationships are formed, lives are shared, and Holy Spirit led prayer for one another's needs is the norm. These groups have helped hundreds of pastors over many hard spots in their personal lives and ministries, but they have done much more. The groups are purposely diverse, mixing cultural backgrounds and various belief streams of the church. Growing in depth of relationship as brothers in the Lord has torn down many walls in the body of Christ and has set a firm foundation of relationship on which many good things have been built in the area.

March for Jesus

Another indirect result of the Davis' trip to Istanbul seemed like an interesting coincidence, but it led to a series of events that changed Austin forever. While there, the Austin team interacted with a team from ICTHUS Fellowship, a church in London that was initiating an interdenominational event where Christians joined to march through the streets, singing praise songs to the Lord. Dan went to London to visit the church and brought back the story of March for Jesus. When Dan shared about the March with Tom Pelton, associate pastor at Family Worship Center in South Austin, Tom picked up on it in a big way. He too visited London, resulting in his becoming the leader in the Americas for the March for Jesus. His American base was Austin, and his main support group was the same group of pastors that would go on to form Pastors in Covenant in years to come. "The first praise march took place in May of 1990. Nine months later, the second march took place in Austin—more than 15,000 came together to praise God in the streets of Austin. Within six months, the USA ministry of March for Jesus was established in Austin with more than 100 cities joining the march across the nation."[2]

Dan Davis had invited Steve Hawthorne to the second march, still called a Praise March. Steve's unique perspective shows a lot about God's heart and about the purpose for the March for Jesus. Steve's account of the day:

> Dan had told me, "I think you need to be part of a local church. I think you should consider Hope Chapel. Why don't you come visit us on March 23, 1991? We're having what we are calling a Praise March, and it would be great for you to see that." So I went and I told God, "If I can contribute something to this, then I'll move to Austin."

Saturday morning I was out there. Arrangements had been made long before for a permit to walk up Congress Avenue to the Capitol. There had been an issue with the permits, because the Texas Stock and Rodeo Show had just swung into town and planned to go up Congress as they always did with all the longhorns. A couple of weeks before they said, "Oh, we need a permit." The city said, "No you can't have the permit, because this religious group is already there." "No, we have television and everything, so just make those religious people go away." "No, we won't."

We had the permit, so the rodeo people had to do it earlier in the day, and they had to go the opposite direction, because there was some sort of issue about the parking. So we all expected we were going to run into longhorns. No one saw a single bovine that day, but we stepped over evidence that they'd been there.

So we lined up on 2nd or 3rd Streets and turned north up Congress. Fifteen thousand people showed up. I'm reading Psalm 68 as we turned the corner: "Arise, O God, let Your enemies be scattered . . . the maidens are in procession with you . . . He rides on the highest heavens . . . We are ascending and coming to your mountain. A mountain of God is the mountain of Bashan." I thought of Psalm 22, the bulls of Bashan. We were just simple maidens in procession, and God was rising, and His enemies were scattered. They were like smoke blown away. That was astounding to me.

After the event, everyone liked it and was amazed at how many different churches had shown up. For Tom Pelton, that was his test day. In Tom's mind, if this was going to fly, then he had already planned that he was going to start a March for Jesus office and work with the people in Britain. He was going to build momentum off this. I met Tom afterwards, and he invited me to come to the meeting of the pastors.

In the meeting, everyone was having a great time, but there was perplexity, "What was this?" "What did we just do?" "What was it?" It wasn't a political thing. It wasn't an evangelistic thing. Why would we have done it? It was a good thing, but we had no category. I thought, "I know what it is." So I told them the Psalm 68 thing. Basically, as we are in procession with our God, He's exalted and it's an entirely different magnitude of spiritual warfare. The Spirit of God was in the room and just clinched it. "That is what we've done. And his enemies were scattered. We've done a beautiful thing for You, Lord."

It was a year later when we saw in John 12, "Leave her alone. She's done a beautiful thing for me." Wearing that anointing, He would go into procession to Jerusalem. It was just a beautiful thing for Him. That truth Tom Pelton would reinforce time and again. He'd say, "Why are we doing this? I think God just likes it." You realize that is enough. *Pretty soon it was just for an audience of one—a choir of millions for an audience of one.*

Shortly after that meeting, I realized I'd told God, "If I can contribute to this, I'll move to this city." I had contributed to it. Tom Pelton's team didn't know how to identify what they'd done. "Lord, You showed me. I was just reading Your word, and You showed me."

The next day I was teaching at Round Rock Fellowship. I had selected the text of the day, which happened to be Palm Sunday, so I opened up the text. As I read it, I had this sense of awe—I was there, I did that. How did I get in the Bible? That's what we were doing yesterday. So we marched with Jesus on Palm Sunday. Just the awe of that shaped a big chunk of who I am and what I do. It really is Palm Sunday. From that time I began to explore the event.[3]

On October 1991, from Austin, March for Jesus was incorporated for the national organization. By 1993 March for Jesus (MFJ) brought 1.7 million Christians to the streets in 850 cities across the globe.

MFJ was a watershed type event that gave birth to a number of other God moves. Leaders of the city had to pull together for March for Jesus in ways they had never dreamed of. Since Austin was the hub for the Americas, leaders came in from all over the nation and the world to plan future marches. Locally, pastors worked together across denominational and color barriers. Intercessors and praying people of all sorts came out of their prayer closets and joined efforts to bathe the event in prayer for months in advance. The Body of Christ rose up and joined hands in unprecedented ways to bless the Lord and the city.

Through the late eighties and the nineties, the Lord built His church in Austin. *As He gave vision to leaders to work toward unity through praise and purpose rather than doctrine, networks of relationship formed, which would lay the foundation for the next century.* However, for Austin's minority people, the foundation through relationship is a whole different story.

Questions to consider:
1. Can you identify catalyst people and groups in your community—those who seem to have vision and have the inner thrust to pursue their vision?

2. If you can name the people or groups, can you identify pieces of vision emerging from these people?

3. What do you see in your city, based on genuine relationship, which challenges division and brings pockets of unity? What has done that in the past? What is doing it now?

4. Look for the bright spots. Rather than focusing on what's wrong with your city, give attention to the positive things that seem to be working, and try to find out why they are working.

5. Ask yourselves how you can build on the positive.

END NOTES
1. Wherever Dan Davis is quoted in this book, it is either from personal interviews or from quotes, used by permission, from an unpublished manuscript that he was working on.
2. "The History of the March for Jesus" an unpublished article written by Cindi Vana, Operations Manager for March for Jesus
3. From an interview with Steve Hawthorne on June 27, 2012

Chapter 5

THE DEEP SOIL OF
RELATIONSHIP

For a city to be transformed, there must be ever increasing unity among people of faith. True unity is not possible apart from trust, and trust grows out of real and sincere relationships. That type of relationship has been growing in Austin in the past twenty years, and the fact that it has is testimony to the amazing grace of God.

This city has not been known for tolerance and love among pastors. A unique exception in early years was birthed out of the worst extreme of intolerance—the treatment of African Americans. In the aftermath of the Civil War, Texas implemented Jim Crow laws, meant to keep the black population in a position of servitude. The city offered utilities to African-Americans only if they lived east of what is now Interstate 35. Out of the darkness of the oppression of the black community, God brought forth a unique expression of transforming relationship.

African-American pastors across the nation have held their communities together, making their churches refuges where respect and relationship protected a glimmer of hope. Dr. Joseph C. Parker, Jr., senior pastor of David Chapel Missionary Baptist Church, says that from the time of the Civil War, black pastors were the only free African-Americans in the South, to the extent that they didn't depend on white people for their living. Because of their unique position in being primarily supported by other African-Americans, they became the spokesmen for their communities. The crucible of segregation and oppression forged a type of unity and interdependence, within their congregations and among the pastors, not found in most Anglo communities. Their utter dependence on God and on community produced the strength of character and unity—based on relationship—that changed the nation through the Civil Rights Movement.

Early seeds of faith

Long before the Civil Rights Movement, seeds of faith and fortitude had begun to grow. In Austin, Jacob Fontaine, an educated ex-slave, led the way in forging a foundation for the black community to build on. Fontaine founded six churches in Austin. "He became active in Republican and Greenback party politics during Reconstruction, operated a grocery, laundry, book, and medicine store. In 1876, he established the Austin Gold Dollar, a black weekly newspaper and the first newspaper under black ownership in Austin."[1] He also helped form what became the St. John Regular Missionary Baptist Association, which still serves the African-American community.

Fontaine epitomized an important aspect of the black church in Austin and other places. The holistic expression of faith cares for the needs of the whole person as well as the society in which that person lives. Because no one else looked out for the needs of the African-American community, black churches banded together to do so.

The St. John Regular Missionary Baptist Association grew in strength and influence. According to the Reverend G. V. Clark, pastor of Mt. Zion Missionary Baptist Church and the current moderator of the association, the early founders chose benevolence, mission, education, and evangelism as the main endeavors of the association. In 1893, when Dr. L. L. Campbell, pastor of the Ebenezer (Third) Baptist Church, became the association's moderator, he negotiated plans for an Orphan Home and School. He purchased 350 acres of land located where Highland

Mall presently sits.[2] The area became known as the St. John's Encampment. Along with the orphanage, which was built in 1906, the encampment also became home to a yearly camp meeting, held every July. Reverend Clark reflected, "Folks would drive in. They'd bring cows to milk, chickens to lay eggs and put up tents and stay the entire two weeks. They'd bring resources to commit to the purposes of the association. I marvel at what our forefathers did. The only thing I can attribute that to is the love of God and commitment to the cause. People would come and stay two weeks, preaching and teaching, being in fellowship, praising God, thanking God, and giving. Sometimes people would pledge bales of hay or a calf or some grain or a percentage of their share crop." The prayer, music, and preaching was coupled with counseling for finding jobs, dealing with economic issues, and other practical aspects of personal life.

The last camp meeting was held on that site in July of 1956. After economic struggles, vandalism, and legal issues, the association finally sold the property and bought the site of the current Tabernacle on Blessing Avenue. Reverend Clark remembers the solidarity of days gone by with a touch of sadness. Although the main endeavors of benevolence, mission, education, and evangelism remain, he doesn't see the same commitment to the work of the association. Though times have changed, the holistic approach to faith and life is still reflected throughout much of the culture of black churches.

A modern look at holistic faith

"Going beyond the walls of the church" and "missional living" are current catch phrases that actually have their roots in holistic thinking. Many black pastors have been taking responsibility for their communities as well as their congregations for decades. It isn't the next move of God for them; it's how they were raised.

Reverend Parker was forged in the fires of Birmingham, Alabama, where his father, Joseph C. Parker, Sr., was a pastor and instrumental in the Civil Rights Movement alongside his college schoolmate, Martin Luther King, Jr. God's command to Jeremiah to "seek the peace of the city" (Jeremiah 29:7) is the driving force of

Joseph Parker, Jr.'s life and ministry. When he heard about a pilot project the city was offering for urban development, he applied for it on behalf of the Chestnut neighborhood, where David's Chapel is located. Pastor Parker, who is also a lawyer, spent over a year visiting people and building trust in the neighborhood. He brought together the local neighborhood associations, provided leadership for them to draw up a plan for neighborhood revitalization, and then raised up leadership from within the group, so it could continue in the execution of the plan with less and less of his input. He also spent many hours at city council meetings seeking equity for the community. The result is a cleaner, safer, more desirable, and more functional neighborhood and a new level of pride and unity among the people who live there.

While Reverend Parker carries a passion for social justice for everyone, Bishop Sterling Lands, pastor of Greater Calvary Bible Church, is known for his passion to educate young people. In 2001, the Eastside Social Action Coalition, led by Bishop Lands, threatened to pull African-American children out of the Austin Independent School District and educate them in local churches if the district didn't do a better job of educating their children.

That wasn't an idle threat. Pastor Lands' heart cry is for all people, especially kids, to have the opportunity to become all they were created to be. While he has put a lot of effort into curing problems, he prefers preventing them. He believes that is best done by working with people from the time they are very young. "It's easier to form the right belief systems than it is to change the wrong ones." He has two schools in his church and a Saturday program called "Rites of Passage." "Rites of Passage" mentors kids from five to eighteen years old. Pastor Lands says, "We deal with competency and character, discipline, attitude, culture, and choice. We have very specific lessons that teach them how to make choices, how to manage anger, how to solve problems. We teach them how to study, how to take tests, how to read paragraphs to know what it really says, how to write." In short, they deal with the whole child to prepare him or her to succeed in every area of life.

These two pastors are living examples of holistic faith. They take missional living to the next level. That's what happens when men and women, regardless of skin color, take the passion God has placed within them, and apply it to every aspect of life. When they do that, transformation happens.

The struggle continues

In modern Austin, the Jim Crow laws are gone. African-Americans can live anyplace they can afford. That doesn't mean the battle against prejudice has ended. It hasn't, but two significant strides were made in the late nineties. The last one was in 1998 when then Mayor, Kirk Watson, called together a group of leaders from a wide-faith base to draft a "Commitment to Racial Reconciliation" in response to a racially charged police event in the city. That document declared the equality of the races and the evil of racism. This document used much of what had already been worked through by a small group of Christian pastors and their wives in 1996 in writing the "Pastoral Covenant for Racial Reconciliation."

The "Pastoral Covenant" grew out of some deep heart searching. When an Anglo pastor asked Joseph Parker to sign off on a commitment that would require marriage counseling before performing a wedding, Reverend Parker replied, "That's fine, but the issue I have is that the only time I hear from my fellow pastors, who are white on the west side, is when they want me to join in on one of their issues. Rarely do they come and join in on any of our issues."

That led to a group of four pastors working together to see what could be done about it. The team consisted of Pastor Geno Hildebrandt, Anglo pastor of North Austin Christian Church at that time, now of Hope Chapel; Pastor Rick Randall, also Anglo, whose church, Austin Cornerstone, sits among the black and Hispanic churches on the east side of Highway 35; Pastor Parker and Ashton Cumberbatch, a lawyer, pastor, and civic leader, both of African-American descent; and their spouses. Ashton Cumberbatch described the document: "It took a year. It acknowledged that racism is a sin and set out some scriptures that supported that. It said we have fallen short of the glory of God in that area, and it talked about things we could do in our individual congregations, and what we could do collectively to combat that. We presented our document to a larger group that existed at the time—Austin Pastors Prayer Fellowship. They thought there was merit, so we had a signing event. I think originally 65 to 70 pastors signed the document."

The "Pastoral Covenant for Racial Reconciliation" was an important step toward reconciliation and renewal. It provided the forerunner breakthrough that made it possible for greater things to follow. The Pastoral Covenant was possible because the men and women who created it already knew something about forging relationship across racial lines.

The power of relationship

One of the most significant examples of such a relationship began during the preparation for March for Jesus in the mid-nineties. Rick Randall describes the event this way:

"A West Austin decision was made for March for Jesus to start over there and march across the highway in symbol of our racial solidarity. None of the churches of color were signing up. Tom Pelton contacted Randy Wallace to sell it to the black pastors. Randy got permission to talk to the Baptist Union Ministers meeting, and Randy asked me to go with him.

He made the presentation. When he was done, I heard this booming bass voice behind me. He said, 'Let me tell you why I'm not interested in March for Jesus. Number one, because you're declaring something that's not true. We are not unified. There's a deep divide racially in our city. Number two, I'm not interested in a photo opportunity. One day you're going to all come together and get a picture. When will I see you again? I'm not interested in a photo op. I'm interested in relationship.'

I stood up and turned around and said, 'I want what you want.' And that was the beginning of my relationship with A. W. Mays (pastor of Mount Sinai Missionary Baptist Church). We decided we'd just meet with no projects for a year, so that anything we did would come out of relationship."

That relationship has become what Ashton Cumberbatch calls a microcosm of some of the things going on in healing of the city. When a close member of Reverend Mays family wanted premarital counseling, he came to Rick Randall to do the counseling, and Pastor Randall performed the ceremony. When Pastor Randall's dad died, Pastor Mays traveled to San Antonio and delivered a prayer at the service.

When Pastors in Covenant groups were started a few years later, Pastor Randall was in a small group made up of five African Americans and three Anglos. The Saturday Pastor Randall's son died, three of those black pastors arrived at his house late at night and sat up with him until Rick could finally fall asleep. They all had church services to conduct the next day, but people in real relationship are there when a brother is hurting.

Building from relationship, Pastor Randall and Pastor Mays joined with two Hispanic pastors, Abram Perez, Ebenezer Family Church, and Lyndon Rogers, Principe de Paz Christian Church, and chose a square mile they called the Windsor Window. They joined their people to form teams to visit everyone in the area. The Windsor community is a broad ethnic mix. By having ministry teams made up of Anglo, African American, and Hispanic mix, they found no one to whom they weren't prepared to minister, and they faithfully reflected God's love for all people. Pastor Randall observed, "The era of Anglos designing programs, bringing them to our brothers and sisters of color, and expecting them to embrace them is behind us. It doesn't work on the mission field, and it doesn't work in our communities either."

Strategies that work are built upon the type of relationships that know and respect one another's gifts and callings. They come out of common vision and purpose that are God ordained and nourished by authentic relationship.

The paradox of success

There is thoughtfulness and a wistful tone in these leaders of the black community as they talk about the road they've traveled. The things they fought for, desegregation and equity, have a byproduct they didn't foresee. The upwardly mobile African-Americans are leaving the East Side. They are now dispersed throughout the city. With integration of the schools, many black teachers lost their jobs and had to move to find new jobs. That meant the role models for less advantaged African-American children were no longer in their schools or on their streets. And for those who have left, there's often a nicer house, a more attractive neighborhood . . . and a loss of community. For community, they drive back across town to the black churches where there are still roots of relationship that keep life grounded. But it's different, and black pastors are challenged. They not only have to pastor their own flocks, they have to redefine what it looks like to pastor the community around their churches.

A new way of seeing

The redefining of community did not catch God off guard. He is raising up a new generation of African-American pastors who are viewing their ministries from a different perspective. Gaylon Clark, Pastor of Greater Mount Zion Baptist Church, sees the community and the city, as well as his local congregation, as his parish. He sees himself as being placed there by God for such a time as this. "We believe passionately in the sovereignty of God, and that God put us on this corner to do what He told us in the scripture, which is to love our neighbors. So we are very passionate about loving those who have proximity to us, and we believe that proximity is God ordered. It's not accidental. It's not incidental. It's very intentional. We minister very passionately to our neighbors. There are African-Americans neighbors; there are Latino neighbors; there are white neighbors; and we want to minister to all of them."

For Greater Mount Zion, loving their neighbors involves helping meet their needs in real ways. The church forms almost everything it does around "8 Great Causes": poverty, health, single parenting, disengaged men, fatherlessness, education, economic empowerment, and teen pregnancy. They plan six outreaches a year to meet community needs in one or more of those areas. Between outreaches, you can find the Greater Mount Zion people doing everything from mentoring kids at Keeling Middle School (a neighbor to the west), to working in neighboring apartment complexes, to providing tests for HIV/AIDS.

For Pastor Clark, loving his neighbors has nothing to do with ethnicity. It has to do with honoring his Lord's commandment. However, he feels specifically called to develop male leaders in the black community:

> I think manhood in our culture is in jeopardy. I want to be part of training a whole new generation of men to lead churches. I want to disciple the next generation *of leaders*. I don't want to disciple someone who's going to go home and take care of his wife and kids and his two-hundred-member church and not really care about the community.
>
> This is where integration messed us up. Our people left the community, and as they left, they adopted white views of life—western views. As we moved out into suburban America, here's what we learned to do: go to work, drive back to the suburbs, click our garage door opener, go in, and take care of our own. So even though our churches are still reaching out holistically, there's no sense of community that brings all the churches together— nothing big enough to drive the pastors together. In the Civil Rights Movement, we didn't have any choice as to whether we were going to work

together. The issues were too big—the challenges too large. We either worked together or we perished together. We don't see that broad collaboration we've had in the past, but we have to find it again. We have to understand we are still at war. Now we must war for the next generation of men in this culture.

The enemy attacks our God-given gifts. It is no surprise that a group of people, created to live in community with strong interpersonal relationships, should be plagued with fatherlessness. How better to destroy a body than to cut off its head?

But Pastor Clark is seeing a few of his fellow pastors take the next step toward collaborating. They are beginning to see the impact they can make on community needs when they join forces.

As the black community redeems their gifts of relationship and holistic faith, they will become contagious. Pastor Clark's people live all over the city, just as do the members of most of the African-American churches. On the one hand, that makes forming viable community more difficult. On the other hand, it positions them to be salt and light to the rest of the city.

Relationship is one of the major keys in transforming a city, but each culture has its own issues to overcome. In the next chapter, we'll look at the Hispanic challenges.

Questions to consider
1. Where are the authentic relationships that cross ethnic and color lines in your community? What relationships in your life space cross ethnic/color lines? How deep are they? How do they enrich your life?

2. What gifts, callings, and vision do you see in ethnic communities that you aren't part of? How can you honor and encourage what you see there? How does what they do bless the community and connect/enhance your work?

3. Begin to ask God to show you a broad spectrum of His Body. You may have a particular view of what you consider to be important, probably born out of your personal understanding and experience. Considering all the aspects of Jesus' earthly ministry, begin to make note of who is filling places that you aren't called to fill. How can you honor them?

4. Look for those from different cultures who seem to have similar vision and calling to yours. Are there ways you could partner with them to increase the effectiveness of both of you?

END NOTES
1. http://www.tshaonline.org/handbook/online.
2. http://www.stjohnbaptistassociation.org/?page_id=17.

Chapter 6

A PASSIONATE PEOPLE

P eople of Spanish descent settled in Texas well before Stephen Austin brought in the first Anglo settlers. In the 2010 census, we see that 35 percent of Austin's population is Hispanic. Most come from Mexico, but many come from other places in Latin America. Some have deep roots here; many do not. If they are a couple of generations removed from their native countries, chances are they understand Spanish, but probably don't speak it.

Jorge Sanchez, who has worked with thousands of immigrants through Cristo Vive, classifies Austin Hispanics by how many generations they've been in the States. He says if their family has been here more than two generations, they are largely embedded in the American culture and have little interest in looking back. The second group—those who are children of immigrants or came as children—is bilingual. They tend to preserve the culture of their native land, but they reach out and make the most of their new world. The third group, made up of first generation immigrants, speaks mostly Spanish and embraces the culture of their homeland. Pastors from each of these categories have shared their stories and beautifully illustrate the big hearts and passionate faith of the Latino pastors in our city.

Anastacio Rodriguez, pastor of Iglesia Camino del Rey, came to Austin in 1996. As many other first gen pastors have done, he started having church with his own family in his own home. "The first year, because we had no people, what we did was just go around the city and pray. We prayed and prayed and asked for the salvation of the people."

The small-home churches give a sense of family and community to many immigrants who have moved far away from their roots. People come and find there is a place to be cared for in a community that understands them—not only their language, but also their culture. They begin to bring their friends and people they work with, and a home group outgrows the garage or living room they are meeting in. Sometimes they rent a storefront. Sometimes they find an established church that will rent them space for afternoon or evening services.

Pastor Rodriguez was one of those. He put a big map of Austin on the wall of his made-over garage that said "Austin for Jesus." He and his family gathered there to pray over it. He recalled, "We were very passionate to do something for Austin. It was my first call to pray for our city. Then I met some other passionate intercessors for Austin and started meeting regularly with them. We found we needed to be more unified. We just met everywhere—in a restaurant or a church late at night with other pastors. There were others starting churches in those days—Lyndon Rogers, Marivel Reyes, Anibal Ramirez, Abraham Perez, Alberto Duran, and some others. We met once a week and prayed. I visited most of the pastors in their homes. I was very interested in bringing them together. We invited them to come together to pray for the city."

Most of the praying pastors Pastor Rodriguez mentioned had already begun praying with one another after working together on March for Jesus. The March greatly impacted the Hispanic community. The language barrier, which often causes a sense of exclusion for the Latin community, wasn't a problem there. The songs were translated into Spanish, and Hispanic churches took part in dance teams, prayer groups, and many other aspects of the preparation.

The best byproduct of MFJ in the Hispanic community was the cooperation it brought among the Hispanic pastors. The group Pastor Rodriguez was praying with found a lot of passionate pastors and intercessors who wanted to do something in Austin. That prayer movement was capped by two larger city events. The group rented Central Christian Church, where three hundred people met on October 28, 1996, to worship and pray and then walk over to the Capitol to pray for the city. After that, they rented a place at Concordia University where a thousand Christians, including fifty pastors, met to pray on April 19, 1997.

Pastor Rodriguez' church outgrew the garage years ago. They are now making plans to build their own church, but the thing that hasn't changed is his commitment to prayer. Around thirty of his congregants meet to pray at 6:00 a.m. Monday through Saturday. They've been doing that for years.

Abraham Perez, pastor of Iglesia Centro Familiar Ebenezer (Ebenezer Family Church), is an excellent example of a child immigrant. He was born in Mexico; his family moved to the United States when he was ten. He speaks good English, but he preaches and does his radio program in Spanish. He feels called to pastor, not just his church, but also his community. Located across the street from Regan High School, he meets the community where its needs lead him.

The church acted as a distribution center and place of refuge after Hurricane Katrina. When a fire swept through the Westheimer Regency Apartments, located near the church, Pastor Perez talked to some pastor friends and announced the need over the radio. A television station picked up the story, and the city responded with non-stop donations. Forty-three churches and organizations worked together to put 145 people in fully furnished apartments in a very short time.

Ebenezer houses a Pregnancy Resource Center, offering free pregnancy tests and sonograms. "We have a boutique here, and we give clothes to newborn babies and also to the mothers. We give formula and Pampers for the babies. We promote life. We try to pray for and witness to the young girls and their families."

This congregation also works to help people become employable. They offer computer classes and classes in English as a Second Language. They teach electrical and plumbing skills and help get their students certified. Several ministries that reach out and meet community needs use the facility.

Pastor Perez explained, "I used to be very involved in the city as far as pastors' events. I used to coordinate and engage pastors in that. In various times I've been led to do different things. From the experience I've had, I felt like I needed to focus on this for now. Build a church that not just meets on Sundays and Wednesdays, but build something that would be more involved with the community. We're building a model to replicate. I will come back to joining with other pastors later to use the model. The idea is not just for me or for this church. The idea is to go through all the learning, go through all the process, and then I want to connect all our resources to enable other churches that want to do the same thing. The ultimate goal is to reach people for Christ and to make disciples. We exist and do what we do only to win souls and make disciples, using every resource God gives us to reach out to people. The idea is to be a model and help other churches do the same thing."

Pastor Perez represents the large numbers of Hispanics who were born elsewhere, and came to the States as children. Commonly, a child born in the States to Latin parents is referred to as second generation. Bishop Paul Ojeda, head of Austin Powerhouse, describes it this way:

> There's a big difference between being 1st and 2nd generation Hispanics. First generation—their way of thinking is for Mexico. They come to Austin, but they still speak Spanish. They just brought Mexico and planted it here. We are a lot different. We don't speak Spanish. We don't speak enough to hold a conversation. I'm 44. My mom grew up when there was a lot of prejudice. When she went to school, she was reprimanded for speaking any Spanish, and if she had any kind of accent, she was looked down on. So when we were growing up, her mentality was that her kids were not going to go through what she went through, so her kids were

not going to speak Spanish and were not going to have an accent. They are going to be American and that's that. My folks only spoke Spanish when they didn't want the kids to understand. So now, years later, you pick up the phone, and it says push one for English and two for Spanish, but it hasn't always been like that, so you have a whole generation who were taught not to speak Spanish, and the only people who do came from over there.

I understand that better, because my wife is from Brazil. She was born and raised in Brazil, so now she gets mad because our kids don't speak Portuguese, and she can never understand me. She will say, "How do you not speak Spanish? You're Mexican." I say, "No, I'm not Mexican, I'm American." She says, "No, you're Mexican." "No, I'm Mexican-American." I don't speak like that or think like that. It's a totally different mentality.

I have about 1,000 members in my church, and a lot of people who are drawn to me are second generation Hispanics who have a similar cultural experience. We're not Mexican. We're not American. We're just kind of stuck in the middle. First generation people find us a little offensive, because we've betrayed the culture, because we don't continue the Spanish language. What we do in this church, once we get them here, is we say, "It's not a black thing or a white thing or a brown thing; it's a God thing." Our whole church knows that saying. When you become a believer, it's the blood that makes us all one, 'cause there's one body, one baptism, one faith, so we don't see through the eyes of culture and man and flesh, we see through the eyes of Spirit, and Spirit sees things completely differently. He sees souls.

So Bishop Ojeda has a different challenge. His people relate with the American culture, and they aren't poor, but there is a deep root of commonality that affects the belief and behavior system of most Latin Americans regardless of how long they have been here. It goes way back.

The Spanish came to the Americas as conquerors during the time of the Spanish Inquisition. They forced their religion upon the natives along with their social system. Religion is one thing—the state of the heart is quite another. The indigenous people had their own gods and their own customs, but rather than die for their beliefs, they simply incorporated them under the cover of Catholicism. Over the centuries distinctions became blurred. Bishop Ojeda said, "We literally have people who come in and go to church, and after they leave church, they go see the witchcraft lady." Superstitions and traditions create a form of religion that has little to do with relationship with Jesus.

Bishop Ojeda's own story gives him a unique perspective on what he is dealing with:

> "I died from a cocaine overdose in 1997 and saw the pit of hell.
>
> I was born in Austin but raised mostly in Houston. I was baptized in Cristo Rey Catholic Church. We were drive-by Catholics.
>
> My wife and I met in drug rehab in 1997 in Houston. After we got out of the rehab, we got worse. So when I died on the cocaine overdose, I saw a black tunnel and started racing to the pit of hell. As I was headed down, that's where God met me. The Spirit of the Lord came upon me and God asked me, 'Paul, what did you do with the life I gave you?' Before I could answer, big as the sky, my whole life flashed in front of me from childhood up to the point where I was—everything I did in secret and in the open. It was there I realized I'd lived for me,

I was a sinner, and I deserved hell. I couldn't justify my sin anymore, so I told God, 'I want to go back and tell the world there's a heaven and a hell, and there's nothing in between.'

I realized how good God is and how merciful He is, so when I woke up, that's when I started reading the Bible. We went to church. I didn't know religion. I didn't know Baptist, Catholic, and Methodist .... I just knew the God who met me on the way to hell. I'm like the blind man who told the Pharisees and scribes, "If you want answers, you have to talk to Him. I was blind and now I see, and that's all I can tell you."

The God he met on his way to hell brought him back to Austin. "What I see God doing with the Hispanic generation is bringing people back to this city. God brought me back with a different mindset. He restored me, healed me, and brought me back to make an impact on the community, because I think the people that stayed, stayed within the four walls and think a certain way, and still live under cultural and generational curses."

To help others find a new mindset, Bishop Ojeda has introduced a strong discipleship program at Austin Powerhouse Church called "Circle of Life." It includes life groups to give people ongoing support, a weekend of ministry called Encounter, and a School of Leadership geared to turn baby Christians into leaders. The Circle of Life has a lot to do with why Austin Powerhouse has grown from ten to a thousand members in only eight years. The Encounter weekend deserves special attention. It is a well-designed weekend that deals with bondages of all sorts. Bishop Ojeda described it like this:

Encounter has been a powerful tool for us. I think what really makes it successful is the preparation, which is the fasting and praying beforehand. We get the names of the participants and pray for

them. In doing that, I believe a lot of strongholds
and generational curses are broken beforehand.
The prep time is the best time. Fajitas are only
good when they marinate for a while; it's the mar-
inating that makes it happen. We've seen lesbians
and homosexuals come in and leave delivered and
healed. We've seen people come in with addictions
and leave free. We've seen people in affairs repent
and go home and restore their marriages.

The leaders fast and pray the Monday through Friday before
the Encounter. Three of those days are water only. The motto of
these committed leaders is: "Someone did it for us."

It is that passionate commitment to the heart of God that
has repeatedly impressed me about the Hispanic people. They
are willing to pay the price. Anastacio Rodriguez' people pray
every morning at 6:00 a.m. When they had their own facility, they
prayed all night every Friday night. Abraham Perez prays with
a group of his people from 5:00 to 6:30 every morning. Marcos
Noriega, leader of Ministerios Roca Eterna, heads up nine congregations in the Central Texas area. Each location prays two to
five mornings a week, some as early as 3:00 a.m. When I ask
Pastor Noriega if he believed God had put an unusual call upon
the Hispanic people to pray more than normal, he laughed, "I
believe God is calling everybody to pray. I've been trying to give
my people a different definition of what is 'normal.'"

Bishop Ojeda said of his second generation Hispanics, "We're
not Mexican. We're not American. We're just kind of stuck in the
middle." I sense that God sees that as a positive thing. The more
I talk to people of different racial groups and different Christian
streams, the more convinced I am that God has a special place
and a unique love for each one—that each group, like each individual, carries an expression of God's character that He values
highly. As for Hispanics, I see these warm-hearted, consecrated,
passionate Latinos as a joy to the Lord's heart. After all, His heart
is in the middle. What a place to be stuck!

Questions to consider:

1. What is the ethnic makeup of your community?

2. What traditions and culture belief systems affect each community?

3. Who are the influencers in those communities?

Chapter 7

"MY HOUSE SHALL BE CALLED A HOUSE OF PRAYER"

In the mid-nineties, when Laura Rarity, a lady who helped build the prayer structure to support March for Jesus, called together a Hispanic group to pray for Latino pastors in the city, she thought her group was the only one praying for Austin. While visiting pastors, she discovered Dr. Estevan Solis, pastor of Iglesia de Dios Unida, a gentleman in his mid-eighties. While she was explaining their purpose, tears started rolling down Pastor Solis' cheeks. He told her that he had been praying for Austin for forty years and that the Lord had promised him that He wouldn't take him home "until the next torch of prayer had been ignited." Then the Lord told Laura He had always had someone praying for Austin.

Prayer is something that usually takes place in quiet, private places, so there is no way of knowing the multitude of prayers that have gone up for this area, but there are some notable examples. One group was an order of Catholic nuns, called the "pink ladies," because they wore pink habits. These nuns prayed 24/7 in Tarrytown from the mid-fifties to the mid-eighties. From the corner of Exposition and Westover, prayer for Austin never ceased for over thirty years.

On December 8, 1941, the day after the Japanese attacked Pearl Harbor, Bishop Clinton Quin, Bishop of the Texas Diocese of the Episcopal Church, called for unceasing prayer during World War II. For the remainder of the war, there was always an Episcopal somewhere in Texas praying for our nation at war. In Austin, Charles Sumners, rector of St. David's Episcopal Church, often took his shift from 2:00 a.m. to 5:00 a.m. Prayer became the centerpiece of Rev. Sumners' life, and St. David's became "an arsenal of prayer."[1] For years, Reverend Sumners held Thursday morning prayer for anyone who wanted to come, making it one of the earliest, if not the first, ecumenical prayer group in the city.

Shifting the atmosphere

According to a great-niece of Reverend Sumners, Bunny Warlen, when Madalyn Murray O'Hare brought her atheist organization to Austin, it so angered Reverend Sumners to have such a thing happen in "his city," that he began walking and praying regularly in the downtown area. He may (or may not) have been the first to take up spiritual arms against the atheist spirit, but he certainly wasn't the last.

Jim Lillard, pastor of House of the Lord, told me: "A lot of people have spent years in prayer, declaration, and prophecy over this city. It is not the center for drug activity, cult activity, and atheist activity that it was in the sixties and seventies." He said, "I'm still as expectant today as I was in 1978 at Brother (Kenneth) Hagin's Camp Meeting[2], when the Lord said to me *'Austin will be known as the revival center of the nation.'*" Pastor Lillard has been declaring that Austin will be known as the revival center for the nation ever since. He has often prayed from a tower overlooking downtown Austin and has fought the negative influences over the city by declaring the truth of God's word, both the written word of the Bible and the prophetic words spoken concerning the city.

In 1982 Jan Wells, an intercessor who later helped establish His Place as a light on 6th Street for a couple of years, was called into the battle. Concerned for the spiritual darkness of the city, she would pray for ministries to come into the city. She remembered:

I'd pray and then talk to spirit-filled ministries. They wouldn't come because they couldn't operate in the gifts in Austin; the darkness was too thick. I began to pray with a couple, and we asked James Robinson to come for a meeting, and he said, "I feel comfortable." So out of that I knew I had to pray for James coming. I went to the Holiday Inn on the river and got a room. While praying I saw the Hilton Hotel, which is now the Holiday Inn, by the old Highland Mall. The Lord told me to go to the Hilton Hotel and start praying, so I got some prayer warriors here in Austin, and we got a room at the Hilton Hotel and just started praying. We were praying for James Robinson and the meetings, when one of the people that worked at the hotel, who knew we were praying, came in and told us that Madelyn Murray O'Hare was there having a meeting. So we began to pray that night against the atheist spirit . . . That night the Lord told me to come to that hotel every month for one year and hold prayer meetings but not to advertise it. So about two months later, when we were praying, that same hotel employee came in and told me the manager had told O'Hare to leave and not come back. She'd been going there for 15 years. We began to see major movement at that time, so we came for one year and prayed over this city, and we walked around the capitol and prayed constantly."

By 1988, when American Atheists, Inc. officially opened its headquarters in Austin, June Criner, a committed intercessor, had taken up the spiritual battle. Through her, God gave this word:

So do you believe I can change the face of a city? Is my power great enough? Yea, I tell you I can move any mountain. I have chosen this place as I have chosen Zion, and I will dwell in it, and many

will come and say, 'Let's go to Austin. You can see
God there. He lives there. You can be healed there,
because God lives there. You can rejoice and praise
there, because God lives there.' I will touch all areas
of this city. None will be untouched. My children will
rise up by My Spirit and by My Wisdom and take
this land that is close to My heart. I will sweep away
all hindrances, not because of anyone, but because
of My Name, and I choose to show Myself strong.
Stand at attention. Wait for the battle cry and then
proceed. It will be beyond your wildest imaginings.
Multitudes of souls will cry out unto My Name from
one end of this city to the other, "JESUS IS LORD!"[3]

Around that time a lady named Joyce Tait, who had been part
of Lydia Fellowship in England, moved to Austin. Lydia Fellowship
had taken seriously the Joshua 1:3 concept of receiving the territory where the soles of your feet tread. Joyce had taken part in
walking the Ring Road in London and claiming that city for God.
When she came to Hope Chapel in Austin, she set up a system of
maps in an old filing cabinet and organized one of the first (pos-
sibly the first) citywide prayer walks called "Walk Austin '88."
John Dawson referred to this effort in his book *Taking Our Cities
for God*:

> One local church in Austin, Texas, spent every
> Saturday afternoon for a year doing prayer walks
> through every section of the city. This practice is
> one of the best ways to gain true understanding of
> the people God has called us to reach. Pray in every
> part of the city and allow God to speak to you there.
> See the whole city as your inheritance.[4]

During the fall of 1989, God prompted men in the jail ministry
team from Mission Hills Church and Hope Chapel to pray for the
city. They gathered to pray weekly. On the night of April 1, 1990,
the Lord led two of them on a four hour "Nehemiah Night Walk"

around the downtown area of Austin between the Travis County jail and the State Capitol. God revealed many things, including "gates" to the city that the Lord said had been established as places of blessing, but which the enemy had used for destruction. That revelation has led numerous small groups to gather in those places to do spiritual warfare and to declare God's purposes of blessing.[5]

For the next ten years, the work around the March for Jesus changed a lot of things in Austin. One of the most significant was to bring pastors together. We'll discuss that in another chapter. Another was to connect prayer leaders in the city. In 1993, Vicky Porterfield volunteered to develop prayer coverage for the next MFJ conference, where organizers gathered from around the United States in Austin to learn more about March for Jesus. Vicky found a few intercessors, mostly strangers to one another, and they grew in numbers and strength and went on to build strong relationships through several years of praying for the annual conferences.

June Criner and Laura Rarity were among the intercessors praying for March for Jesus. They teamed up to form a unique partnership in pulling the city together. Laura's background and gifting uniquely prepared her to build bridges. She is Hispanic with an Anglo husband. She grew up Catholic, learned to love the word of God through Bible Study Fellowship, and was baptized in the Holy Spirit alone in her prayer closet while she searched for more reality in prayer. Because she didn't see or understand the divisive issues, she did all sorts of things one "couldn't do in Austin." She helped pull the Hispanic community together to pray for the city; she drew Catholics and Protestants together; and she, along with June, ignored racial barriers, denominational barriers, Charismatic barriers, and barriers that often arise between pastors and intercessors to help organize worship and prayer gatherings in a diverse variety of churches all over the city.

Probably the most profound of those gatherings was a 24/7 Solemn Assembly called "Tabernacles '98" that June orchestrated during October 4–11, 1998. Worship and prayer didn't stop for a solid week. They felt the *Lord had told them that bringing unity through prolonged prayer and worship would shift the spiritual atmosphere in the city.* It did. Six months later, in April 1999, Ron Barrier, national spokesman for American Atheists, announced that the group was moving its headquarters from Austin, Texas, to Cranford, New Jersey, stating that "the Northeast is much more progressive than the South . . . " (Montgomery Advertiser, 1999, 3-D). They moved that same month.

"Tabernacles '98" seemed to bring the final shift to move the atheists, but God had used many people who walked the streets to pray, who would hear Him and declare His word over the city, and who would worship Him and draw in His presence.[6] These few, I have mentioned, unknowingly worked together to remove the curse of being called the atheist capital of the nation. Each was simply obeying God as He orchestrated their prayers and activities to change the atmosphere of the city.

A new millennium

The twentieth century saw prayer in Austin move from small groups isolated in cloistered places to joyful praise ringing through the streets of the city as men and women of God learned to join forces regardless of doctrine, culture, generation, and gender. The city was ready for a brand new century—indeed a brand new millennium.

The new millennium brought some new faces. A young Catholic man, Daniel Geraci, was, in his words, "a baby Christian," when Cheryl Max of St. Thomas More Catholic Church had a vision to put on an event in a large arena, prior to the Millennium, to celebrate Jesus. Cheryl, Daniel, and a small team managed to reserve the Frank Erwin Center for the event. Prior to that time there had never been a Christian event in the facility, and this one would have been banned but for the help of the American Center for Law and Justice, which intervened at Daniel's request. Over 5,000 people from 200 churches welcomed the new millennium into Austin, lifting up the name of Jesus.

That event jumpstarted a series of citywide prayer meetings that encompassed the city for the next fourteen months. Citywide prayer was another piece in drawing together the prayer force of the Hispanic community. At first, the group of Hispanic pastors, who had been praying together regularly since the March for Jesus days, didn't trust Daniel. Since he was Catholic at that time, they feared he wanted to draw their people back to the Catholic Church. One morning Daniel was headed to Templo Monte Sinai, Pastor Manuel Ramos' church on East Riverside, to talk with some Hispanic pastors about hosting a Citywide Prayer event, when a cement truck ahead of him tipped over and blocked the street. With traffic penning him in, Daniel saw no way he would be able to make his meeting. Then a cab driver from a couple lanes over motioned for Daniel to roll down his window. In Daniel's words:

> The cabbie shouted, "Are you trying to go some-where?" "Yes. I have a 9 o'clock meeting!" He says, "Where?" I shouted back the address, and he said, "Follow me!"

> Suddenly, the sea of stand-still cars parted, and I followed him down many side roads and places I had never driven before, and he got me to the meeting right at 9:00 a.m. I truly believe this person was an angel of the Lord, helping me get to this key pastors' meeting. When I told the pastors the story, they were all amazed and agreed it was of the Lord. We prayed together and talked. Walls melted into friendship, and the prayer meeting at Pastor Ramos' church was one of the largest and most powerful we had.

The Hispanic churches still provide some of the most consistent prayer coverage for the city. Most of the Latin pastors I interviewed lead a group of their people in praying for the city early in the morning at least five days a week. Some of them have been doing that for over ten years.

Jesus Video Project and Sheep Pen 23
During that same time frame, another prayer warrior began to take her place in the community. Barbara Bucklin moved to

Austin with her husband in the mid-nineties. After his death, Barbara became involved in many God-projects and formed Luke 4:18 Ministries. In 2000, while Daniel was forming Citywide Prayer, Barbara became the Texas coordinator for the Jesus Video Project. They mailed the videos throughout about half the city, and then they followed up with a lot of prayerwalking. In zip code 78723, Charlie Lujan, prayer director for PromiseLand Church, used his team of trained intercessors to prayerwalk before evangelistic teams handed out the videos.

Daniel's group and Barbara's group overlapped and joined forces. The Lord gave Daniel the vision for the next step—to target one zip code. They called the project "Sheep Pen 23" targeting 78723, where several of the participating pastors had churches. "One of the things the Lord had us do," recalled Daniel, "was to stake out the zip code." One night, eight or nine of them drove the entire perimeter of the zip code, stopping at every major entry into the area to drive a stake with scripture on it into the ground. They prayed at each "gate" to the community. They finished with communion at 4:30 in the morning. Daniel and Lyndon Rogers, Pastor of Principe de Paz, spiritually mapped the area, making note of crime rates and where the hot spots were. Teams would go out and pray in places where crime was the highest, asking God to transform them. Both Charlie and Barbara developed strong on-site prayer teams that have continued to pray on site in some of the darkest parts of the city. In addition, Lyndon and one of his members walked around a large lot across from Webb Middle School where there was an abandoned nursing home and claimed it for the Lord.

Along with a lot of prayerwalking and on-site prayer, each month they would meet at a different church in the community to pray and worship. Daniel said, "There was a bridge on Manor Road, where underneath there was terrible graffiti and a lot of drugs were done there. We decided to love the area by having a party and repainting it and putting scriptures where the graffiti had been. I got approval for that. The city provided the paint. We had a sign made and put it by the bridge that said, 'We dedicate this zip code to Jesus Christ.' The city approved it. Then we had an event for the whole community where churches came together."

Prayer works! The crime rate went down considerably during 2001. It is also noteworthy that the old Mueller Airport area, located in 78723, has been transformed with Dell Children's Hospital and Mueller Retail Center serving the area. The land Pastor Rogers claimed for God now houses The For the City Center, an outreach of Austin Stone Church, which was planted with the purpose of reaching out to and serving the East Austin community. Other strong churches have relocated into the zip code: El Shaddai is a strong prayer force on the northeast corner where Highways 290 and 183 intersect. Pastor Marivel Reyes has a prayer chapel open 24/7 and leads her people in strategically spiritually mapping their area and praying for the needs they find there.

On the northwest corner of the area (Highway 290 at Interstate Highway 35), sits Austin Cornerstone. Pastor Rick Randall had a dream in which the Lord showed him that if his church were removed, it wouldn't make a ripple in the community. He went to the leaders of the church and said, "We aren't making any difference. We have all these neighbors around us, but we aren't impacting the neighborhood." They created a three-day summit, where they had all the leaders of the church meet. They invited in the police department, the fire department, the heads of the homeowners associations, the managers of all the apartment complexes, the principals of all the schools, and representatives of the city health department and housing, and they asked them all the same question. "Tell us what you see to be the needs of this part of the city." They then adopted a square mile area they called the Windsor Window, and several churches (Anglo, African-American, and Hispanic) joined forces to respond to those needs.

The gates of the city
Another newcomer the Lord sent to Austin was an Anglican from Nigeria, Benjamin Anyacho.[7] In 2002 Benjamin had just finished teaching a series from Psalm 24 about the spiritual gates of

a city, when Bob Long invited Prophet Chuck Pierce to speak at Rally Call Ministries. On June 20, 2002, Chuck gave this prophecy:

> And the spirit of God said, "I am sending a sign of hail upon this state [Texas]" . . . "I'm sending—I'm going to start sending a sign of hail on this state in the next two months. When you see hail fall in your city, know that it is time for the heavens and the atmosphere to change." And He said also, "at that time declare where hell on earth has controlled your city, declare to hell—that the hail from heaven is a change that it is losing, [it] is a sign that it is about to lose its authority in your city. Declare it is a time for change and that everything hell is holding captive in your city, the resources both physical as well as material that have been held back and robbed from the church, declare that both will start being let go. This is a key time. I am changing the atmosphere of heaven even now over this state. Watch for the changing and watch for the signs and move accordingly," saith the Lord.[8]

Benjamin Anyacho was at that meeting. After the prophetic word, Pierce called him up and prophesied over him. Part of that word said that when it hailed, they were to go to the gates of the city. Three days later, when the hail came, Barbara Bucklin called Benjamin, and a group met at Benjamin's house to map out the gates of the city, using information gained by the men who did the "Nehemiah March" ten years earlier. They sent two intercessors to each gate to pray. They continued to pray every Tuesday for eight months for the city.

During the time that Benjamin and Barbara led teams to pray over the gates of the city, Vicky Porterfield was being led in another direction. During a season of personal prayer, seeking God for how to promote prayer in the city, Vicky felt led to start building prayer within the churches. She remembers, "I recognized that I needed a leadership base of people from different backgrounds to reach the many churches. Dan Davis told many area pastors, and I developed a team from Baptist, Charismatic, Presbyterian, Methodist, and Lutheran backgrounds. I called on several pastors and asked to meet their prayer leaders. Unfortunately, many churches had none." Vicky met with her team once a week to build Pray Austin, and they invited teachers in for monthly meetings to train on various aspects of prayer.

Global Day of Prayer

A voice that has shaped the course of unifying prayer in Austin, perhaps more than any other, is Steve Hawthorne. Steve moved to Austin in August of 1991 as a result of his encounter with God at that second praise march. He trained the city in prayerwalking. He co-authored the book *Prayerwalking, Praying on Site with Insight* with Graham Kendrick along with writing numerous books that put scriptural muscle behind the prayers of ordinary men and women who want to pray for their communities. For Steve it is always about ordinary people being focused on an extraordinary God.

Steve has helped organize and train groups for prayerwalking in Austin, around the country, and around the world. Each year he writes a booklet called *Seek God for the City* designed to be used to bless your community during Lent. He also writes the prayer guides for Global Day of Prayer. He helped organize and lead Prayerwalk USA and Austin's piece of that, Prayerwalk Austin. Steve said, "As a subset of Prayerwalk Austin, we did something we called Lite the Night. From Halloween to Thanksgiving we walked a specific area, a seven-digit zip code. Lite the Night was a code name for the event, from the darkness of Halloween to the brightness of thanking God. We asked people to commit to prayerwalk two different areas—one near their home and one in a part of Austin they didn't usually go to. The principle was that we didn't just ask people to take their area at home but to cover more of the area and know their city."

Steve is on the Global Planning Committee for Global Day of Prayer, and the organization he heads, WayMakers, helps provide material and leadership locally as well as nationally for the event. Austin has taken part in GDOP celebrations since 2005. Pastor Lyndon Rogers told of the way the Lord blessed the event in 2007. He described a rainy Saturday, when runners from several churches joined forces to carry a torch around the city. As they ran, the rain would stop where the torch was being carried. When they met on Mt. Bonnell to finish with prayer, the storm was threatening. They prayed, and it stopped and waited until they finished and then came in.

The next day, Pentecost, they gathered in four major racial groups—Asian, Hispanic, Anglo, and African American—to come from four directions and join to take the torch into the Delco Center. At the moment the groups united, a rainbow ring formed around the Delco Center in the sky. It wasn't an arch. It wasn't a bow. It was a ring. Pastor Chang, of the Austin Chinese Church, had seen that happen once before—in China over a baptism service at a secret house church. Pastor Rogers observed, "When we pastors put aside our differences, and those differences become secondary, there's a visitation of Jesus. He approves of that, because we are living out John 17, that we may be one so the world will believe. When we allow division to come between us, it causes that so many don't believe. The efforts to change that are bearing fruit in Austin. When the pastors come together and the communities stand alongside, there's nothing but the blessings of our Lord."

"My house shall be called a house of prayer"

Several houses of prayer have begun and are working toward 24/7/365 prayer in the area. For several years, Austin House of Prayer (AHOP), under the leadership of Thomas Cogdell, has worked closely with Global Day of Prayer to provide around-the-clock prayer for the ten days leading up to Pentecost.

Thomas and his wife, Amy, are called to reconciliation between Catholics, Protestants, and Messianic Jews. They are ordained leaders planning for the 500th anniversary of Martin Luther posting *The Ninety-five Theses* on the church door, which will be in Wittenberg, Germany, on October 31, 2017.

The Campus House of Prayer (CHOP) was born from the prayer womb of Campus Renewal Ministries. Campus Renewal

Ministries was conceived in 1991 with three students meeting every morning at 7:00 a.m. to pray for transformation at the University of Texas. That grew to twelve people, which grew to a weekly prayer meeting involving twenty campus ministries.[9] That simple beginning has produced a movement that unites and mobilizes the various campus ministries, launches missional communities, and provides a prayer force for the campus. It also proves UT's slogan "What starts here changes the world," because it has become a model for campus renewal on other college and university campuses.[10]

The newest of the area houses of prayer is Heart of Texas House of Prayer (HOTHOP) run by David and Bethany Martin. It meets in Leander. Bethany's heart is connection: "When we started Live Worship Capital[11], the first mandate was to connect the houses of prayer. So we've deliberately cross-pollinated. We've gone to Austin House of Prayer. They've come over here. We've connected with Campus House of Prayer—just trying to cross-pollinate and also to connect the worshippers." Bethany, an established worship leader, has made it her goal to connect the worship community and to give young worship leaders a leg up. Her latest CD, "Austin, Texas, Live Worship Capital," features some of the city's best young worship leaders. She feels that lately God has been emphasizing prayer. She says God wants unity among the different thrusts of His people, including worship, prayer, and evangelism. "He said, 'My house shall be called a house of prayer for all nations.' I think it's all of it together. Psalms 133 emphasizes what you get with unity."

Unceasing Prayer

While the houses of prayer are working toward 24/7/365 prayer, a group of churches have joined forces to achieve it. In 2008, during a season of prayer, Trey Kent, pastor of Northwest Fellowship, was prayerwalking in his neighborhood, when he thought about how great it would be if there were always people praying for the city that way. From that, the Lord inspired him to call pastors together to start Unceasing Prayer for the area. Over thirty churches and some ministries have worked together to provide round-the-clock prayer. After a student opened fire with an assault rifle on the UT Campus in 2010, the Lord told one of the Unceasing Prayer coordinators that Colton Tooley didn't shoot anyone (except himself) because Austin was covered in prayer.

Once a dead end for pastors and a bastion for atheists, Austin was a place that ministries avoided, but now they come. Now they even move here. Why? They come because God can change the face of a city. He laid this city on the hearts of ladies in their prayer closets, of pastors prayerwalking their neighborhoods, of college students, and of immigrants. He called leaders from across the nation and the world to bring strategy and fortitude. He broke down walls of prejudice and bias and built bridges of understanding and cooperation to replace them, and that's only the beginning. Yes, God can change the face and the heart of a city, and He uses folks like you and me to do it. It takes a lot of little acts of obedience to build the big picture. What's your piece?

Questions to consider

1. Who is carrying the burden for prayer in your city?

2. Where are the beginnings of unity forming?

3. What has God said about your city? Are you honoring and acting upon the prophetic words He has spoken?

4. What dividing walls have come down, and what ones still need to tumble?

5. How are you recognizing and honoring those who intercede for your city?

END NOTES

1. Fowler, Beth. *The Spirit of Missions*, Book, 2000
   http://texashistory.unt.edu/ark:/67531/
   metapth201190/m1/25/

2. Reference is to Kenneth Hagin, Sr., founder of Rhema Bible College in Tulsa, Oklahoma.
3. Criner, June. "Conquering a City."
4. John Dawson, *Taking Our Cities for God*, (Lake Mary, Florida: 1989), 86.
5. From "Summary of Nehemiah Walks" in an unpublished prayer journal compiled by June Criner.
6. Psalm 22:3 says that God inhabits the praises of His people.
7. You can learn Benjamin's story from his book, Anyacho, Chinedum Benjamin, *Bold Fresh Wine, a Cry for Sustainable Transformation.* AuthorHouse. 2010.
8. http://www.elijahlist.com/words/display_word. html?ID=1225.
9. http://texasunited.org/about/history/.
10. For more information, see Justin Christopher's book: *Campus Renewal, a Practical Plan for Uniting Campus Ministries in Prayer and Vision.* Campus Renewal Ministries (Austin, Texas: 2010).
11. Live Worship Capital is a website designed to support for the worship community. To check it out, go to www. liveworshipcapital.com/.

Chapter 8

SEEKING A BLUEPRINT FOR TRANSFORMATION—ABBA

Shortly before the turn of the century, while God was forming a new way of looking at church in Austin, He was also preparing another important piece from far away. When Bill Bright stepped down from leadership of Campus Crusade for Christ, the new leadership team sought God for direction. They started getting vision for cities as a whole—not just ministries within cities. They brought that concept to the team Alan Nagel was on—the Global Community Resources team. Alan still lived in Austin, but was dealing with cities all over the world. The Crusade leadership asked Alan's team to start thinking conceptually about the whole city, not just about having a ministry in the city. How would you approach a city? Alan's team spent three years as they traveled, processing that and looking at concepts and principles only—not the program. Alan remembered, "We came up with a framework of what would have to be in play if we were really serious about the city. After three years of that and still traveling, I sensed the Lord saying, 'You need a laboratory.'" That was about year two thousand. Alan told how he found his "laboratory":

> In 2001 I ran into Dan Davis at IHOP. I hadn't seen him in eighteen years. When Dan asked what I

was doing with Crusaders, and I told him we were trying to figure out what it would take conceptually to touch a whole city, Dan lit up. He said, "I've got to talk to you. My heart's bleeding for this city. I want to find out what you're learning." I said, "Dan we don't know anything. We just have some principles and concepts."

The next day we spent several hours comparing notes and found we had a lot of the same vision. We realized that God was putting cities on the hearts of leaders. We've been joined at the hip ever since.

Even before the meeting with Alan, Dan had already been connecting with people with "city-reaching vision." Dan and David Dalgleish, a contractor, had been talking for some time, when David Smith, of Austin Baptist Association, connected them to John Berryhill, a church-planting specialist who had been part of Mission Houston before coming to Austin. John brought Bob Sleet, who had been working with Reed Carpenter of the Pittsburgh organization called the Leadership Foundations of America (LFA). At that meeting Bob told them about a group called "Partners In Ministry," part of the LFA, led by Bill Blackburn in Kerrville, Texas. The Austin group scheduled a trip to Kerrville to check out what he was doing. On the drive home, they came up with a basic vision for ABBA.

Along with that beginning vision, Dan told Alan he had an old 501c3 called Austin Bridge Builder's Alliance (ABBA) they could use. Its original purpose was to explore how to meet the needs of the city of Austin through the churches and business leaders. Alan said, "That's only one segment of the city. Are we going for the whole city or are we just going to meet needs?" Dan said, "Let's go rewrite it. We're going for the city."

Movement—not ministry

One of the essential pieces that Alan brought was definition. ABBA was not to be a ministry. ABBA didn't exist to do any specific element of ministering to the city. It wasn't called to feed the poor or educate the children or preach the Gospel. ABBA was called to coordinate the groups that did all those things and many more. This is the way Alan defined the difference: "A ministry addresses an issue or issues and develops the strategies and programs to deal with the issue. A movement is ordained by God to draw into a unified thrust all the moving parts that serve a city. *It moves around principles not programs.* ABBA was planted by God to build bridges that would facilitate a movement of transformation."

Holy Spirit led

Alan said, "It doesn't take long, in trying to deal with the complexities of a city, to realize that the job is impossible. One of the biggest things we have learned is that if it's not impossible, it's not supernatural, and if it's not supernatural, it won't transform anything. Without God at the helm, the best you will have is a program."

We can look back at the forerunner pieces like The March for Jesus and the connecting of the city's intercessors, and recognize God's hand laying foundation pieces even before ABBA was a dream in anyone's head. We have watched the Lord orchestrate and connect pieces over and over again as He unfolds His blueprint for Austin. *It is imperative to look for what the Holy Spirit is doing and move with that.*

Vision and Mission driven

When the team gathered to rewrite the 501c3 for Austin Bridge Builders Alliance, their central focus was to write the vision and mission for the organization. They understood that while there would have to be a lot of flexibility in following the Holy Spirit day by day—making room for pieces He would bring that they didn't even realize were important—they also needed an overriding vision to set a foundation and framework. Without that, it would be too easy to be swayed off track by one compelling piece to the detriment of the whole.

The team God had drawn together carried an interesting mix of city vision. Barbara Bucklin had worked in the prayer movement and had volunteered for or led various organizations addressing the city's needs. Ashton Cumberbatch provided leadership in reconciliation and social justice. Dan Davis had poured his life into the pastors of the city. David Dalgleish carried a business perspective and a gift for catching God's creative ideas. Bob Sleet was a relationship builder who connected a broad spectrum of government, business, and minority interests. Alan Nagel saw a broad scope, which included the necessity of building toward movement while avoiding the limitations of building a ministry. Ron Harris, of Harris Preston & Partners, added a systematic approach of asking the right questions to help the group evaluate and hone in on defining their purpose.

As these leaders, each with his or her particular passion for the city, prayed together, listened to God and to each other, and shared their hearts, they were looking for God's compelling vision.

When the Body of Christ unites
behind a compelling vision and a clear mission,
it becomes the largest resource for good and change in a city!

The vision had to be broad enough to encompass the entire city—to include God's heart and purpose for everyone. It had to be that compelling vision that everyone could get behind.

> ABBA's vision: *"A united Body of Christ, throughout Greater Austin, serving the needs of our city, and its people, such that the city is experiencing the transformational love of God—culturally, socially, and spiritually."*

The vision set the foundation and borders for what they were going after—one united Body that encompassed the entire area, working together to express God's love in every place and every way. Who can connect with ABBA's vision? Anyone who wants to express Christ's love as well as anyone who needs to receive Christ's love. How could that love be expressed? In as many ways as there are human hearts to express it . . . You want to feed the homeless? So does that group over there. Could you do a better job if you worked together? You want to start a hiking club to give a place for relationship to grow? Great idea! There's a church over there that does that sort of thing. They might be able to give you some pointers. You want your church to be part of an evangelical campaign to reach the whole city? The Pastors' Council is working on that. We'll show you where to connect.

A vision sets the bar high. It becomes the North Star toward which the organization navigates. There can be thousands of paths that contribute to the vision. The point is that none of the paths take the place of the North Star. The ministry to the homeless is well within the scope of the vision, but if the vision becomes helping the homeless, to the exclusion of the rest of the city, it has gone astray. The mission statement helps clarify:

> ABBA's Mission: *Connecting the church community and its resources to the needs of the city/region so that every man, woman, and child can see and hear the compelling mission of Christ's love for them.*

The mission statement gives an important guiding key— "every man, woman, and child." Because there are so many needs and causes in a city, it is easy to allow the focus to veer into a particular area to the exclusion of other areas. ABBA's role became to unite the Body of Christ—never embracing any explicit ministry function or assuming a role that another organization was chartered to perform. *ABBA's role is to be a neutral coordinator to incorporate and unite congregations, ministries, businesses, professionals, and others to work together for the greater good.* Their call is to provide the connective tissue to join the parts of Christ's body in the city. Envision the difference between a mission and a movement. It takes many individuals and groups on mission, providing the many body parts that must be in place if the Body is to have movement and to become A Movement.

In ABBA, God added a unique dimension to the city. *He added a neutral facilitator of connection for the entire area.* ABBA set out to unite the whole Body of Christ for the transformation of the whole city. Obviously, declaring such a purpose and fulfilling it are two entirely different things. It requires a lot of buy-in from the Body of Christ. To get that requires looking at things from an entirely new perspective. It's a totally impossible concept except . . . except that it was God's idea, and God is Lord of the impossible. In the next chapter we will see how God opened the door and gave ABBA its place in the city.

After that, we'll look at a few more principles of transformation. To review the principles we have already discovered:

- Transformation is birthed from a movement, not a ministry. It takes many ministries to make up a movement.
- A movement is Holy Spirit led. Ministries can be built on man's ideas, but apart from the direction and anointing of the Holy Spirit, the best man can produce is fairly effective programs. Programs won't transform anything. Only God can do that.
- Transformation moves out of clear God-given vision and mission.

Questions to consider:
1. Who has vision for reaching the city in your community?
2. What vision do these people carry?
3. Ask God who carries the anointing to connect those people of vision.
4. If you were going to call a group of leaders together to pray and seek God's heart for your city, whom would you include?

Chapter 9

TWO STORMS

Sometimes it takes an act of God to break old mind-sets in order to see a larger picture of what God is doing.

As ABBA was struggling to find its identity and then for that identity to begin to be recognized in the city, God had his own way of preparing the city's pastors for a new view of the city. Up until this time, pastors were pretty much wrapped up in their own ministries and saw very little reason to look beyond them.

The Pastors in Covenant (PIC) groups had laid the foundation for relationships among the pastors in the city. They had found the value in being friends, but hadn't seen the need to work together on any kind of consistent basis. According to Tim Hawks, Hill Country Bible Church Austin, some pastors viewed ABBA as one more group asking for time. The pastors didn't know anything about a prototype to connect their strengths to transform a city, but circumstances began to challenge their long-held mindsets of individualism. It took a couple of natural disasters to foster a real breakthrough.

By 2004 some pastors were beginning to see the need for a different type of relationship among themselves and with the city. Hawks told of two early efforts of pastors gathering to consider how to change the negative attitudes of the city toward the church. At the first gathering a group of pastors came together to talk about how to do ministry effectively. One of the pastors was having trouble with the city over a building permit and felt like there was a need for unity to help the city realize the power and value of the church. He said he wanted the city to have a bigger vision. He believed, rather than being antagonistic toward churches, there should be collaboration.

The First Storm

That particular meeting didn't lead to any action, but the time frame is interesting. That was November 2004. On December 26, 2004, an incredibly powerful tsunami wreaked havoc in Indonesia. Even though Indonesia is on the other side of the world, it's significant to Austin because of the response from Austin.

Ron Parrish, then pastor of Hope in the City, already had mission teams in Indonesia. His own family had served there for many years, so when tragedy hit on the other side of the world, he had a team, whose members spoke the language and knew the customs, ready to go. What they needed was money. Rapidly, they collaborated with other churches in the city to raise funds. Hope in the City took a team of doctors, nurses, counselors (some of whom could speak the language), and the support and prayer of the Body of Christ in Austin, Texas. Stories of miracles in distribution and personal care trickled back to the churches that had sent support.

In the meantime, the city of Austin held a walk-a-thon and raised $47,000 to send to Indonesia, which made headlines on the front page of the Austin American-Statesman. One pastor shared his perspective:

> The city did a walk-a-thon to raise money. That's good. The city raised $47,000, and that was a front-page headline in the Statesman. Several churches wrote checks bigger than that, and that didn't hit the front page of anything. Hill Country Bible Austin,

Hope in the City, Grace Covenant, Hyde Park—
churches all over the city were doing things. There
had to be a couple of million dollars of Kingdom
resources and Kingdom expertise that went directly
to aid those people in Indonesia, and nobody knew
about it except the individuals in those churches.

Several pastors felt it didn't make sense for them to be such a
positive influence in the city and have no one know about it. Tim
Hawks called a meeting of a bunch of key pastors in town. At that
gathering, the pastors also asked one another what they should be
doing to coordinate their church activities to work together, so if
something like this happened in Austin, they'd be prepared to meet
the need. One pastor described the meeting: "Everybody sat around
the table. Everybody agreed. We talked, but we never did anything
after that. We just had a meeting."

No one picked up the ball, but questions were raised and mindsets were challenged. Hawks reflected, "The first thing you have
to do to bring change in a city is to unfreeze from the way you are
currently doing things. The American church system is made up
independent blocks that seldom open the door to any kind of collaboration, or even an acknowledgment that other people are doing
things, and we could work together." This meeting didn't move any
mountains, but the acknowledgement of the need opened a crack
of preparation for the next big thing.

The Second Storm

That meeting was early in 2005. Then the next big thing hap-
pened. In August 2005, Hurricane Katrina ripped the shores of the
Gulf Coast and poured thousands of homeless people from New
Orleans into Austin's lap.

When Bob Sleet, then Executive Director of ABBA, heard that
the city had agreed to take thousands of the displaced refugees, he
and his wife Barbara went to the Convention Center, arriving ahead
of the buses of refugees. They volunteered to help. They did everything they could personally, and then, thanks to the relationship Bob

and Ashton Cumberbatch had built with Toby Futrell, Austin's City Manager, they were in a position to connect the church to the need.

It quickly became obvious to city officials they needed help—a lot of help. That was when the third meeting of pastors took place. Dan Davis had the relationship with the pastors. Bob and Ashton had favor with the city. ABBA stood in the middle. Tim Hawks described what took place:

> At that point in time—I don't know who called the meeting—but the churches and ABBA were sitting in a room, and ABBA was saying they would be happy to coordinate the effort, and the churches said, "Perfect." I remember sitting with Sterling Lands in the meeting. He said, "Folks, we need to respond to this, we need to help these folks," and ABBA stood up and said, "We'll help coordinate this thing." That was the moment that the church and ABBA began to understand that there was a way to work together.

Through ABBA there was the organization to pick up the ball to coordinate the resources. Bob Sleet was able to get a number of pastors into Berger Center to serve and minister to the people. Several churches adopted families and helped them find homes. ABBA took responsibility for organizing a way to distribute the tons of clothing and household articles that came from people throughout the area who wanted to help. The city manager arranged for the use of several airplane hangers to house and distribute the donations.

Since the majority of the refugees were African-American, it helped that several black churches were involved. Pastor Ivie Rich, of St. Luke Missionary Baptist Church, became the face of the Austin Disaster Relief Distribution Center. He and Elissa Benford, entrepreneurial owner of Lisa's Hope Chest, worked closely with Sleet to categorize and grade the goods donated. People from over one hundred congregations in the city participated in the sorting and distribution of these goods. The team learned later that in similar situations in other cities, without a way to handle the massive aid donations, goods often degrade in storage and end up in landfills.

Pastor Rich, Bob Sleet, and their team served approximately 3,400 individuals.

Hurricane Katrina's tidal wave into Austin helped define ABBA's place as a credible connector in the area. The walls between government and church were breached to form viable cooperation. Races worked hand in hand to meet needs, and churches joined forces across racial, denominational, and theological barriers to express the love and compassion of Jesus to thousands of hurting people. As the onslaught of need subsided, the idea of cooperation for the good of the city remained, and ABBA emerged as a neutral place where it was safe to connect and serve together.

One pastor referred to the Indonesian tsunami and Hurricane Katrina as "acts of God" to which the church had the opportunity to respond. Another perspective is that whatever God allows, He uses for good for those who love Him and are paying attention to His purposes. However you look at it, God used those storms for good. Natural disasters remove natural barriers and change the landscape. In this case, they also broke down some mental and spiritual barriers and opened the way for a whole new realm of cooperation in the city. In the next chapter we'll consider what that looks like and get a few more lines added to our Blueprint for Transformation.

Questions to consider:
1. Is your city prepared to step into opportunity?
2. What mindsets exist in your churches that stand in God's way of transforming your city? Are some of those in your own life?
3. Can you identify anything God has been doing in your city to challenge isolation-type mindsets?
4. What crises have shaped the relationships in your city? (For good or for bad)
5. What resources exist in your city that, if they worked together, could meet a crisis?
6. What relationships exist within those resources that are strong enough to bring the pieces together?

Chapter 10

EXPANDING THE BLUEPRINT— IN THE CITY FOR THE CITY

A man of peace

Alan Nagel, by this time Executive Director of ABBA, described another of the principles that has guided ABBA:

> In Luke 10 Jesus told His disciples to go into the villages and towns, where He was sending them, and look for "the man of peace." God has His men and women of peace, the ones in whom He has planted vision, all over the place. The challenge is to find them and see how their vision connects to the larger vision. The world's method, of looking for and hiring the most qualified person for the job, just doesn't work for God's impossible tasks. In the first place you are working with an army of volunteers. There isn't enough money to hire the kind of help you need, and if there were, it wouldn't work anyway. You'd end up with a giant program disconnected from the heart of God. No, you have to look for the ones who carry a piece of God's vision and allow Him to show you where they fit.

The man-of-peace principle alone takes some mindset breaking. It requires learning to be at peace with ever-changing vision. God brings new pieces, and then lets each piece struggle over the new relationship. It forces an ever-expanding vision to accommodate a greater scope of diversity. He removes a piece, and the whole vision requires adjustment, because it's built on relationship, not programs.

A prime example is the ebb and flow of something called In the City for the City. In the City for the City was a dream birthed in the heart of David Dalgleish. Dan Davis tells the beginning of the story:

> In a particularly fruitful ABBA planning session, David Dalgleish came up with the idea of an event we would hold in a premier civic center venue called the Bob Bullock Texas State History Museum, located on the Capitol grounds. The idea would be that we would invite all the various ministries that serve our city, including some of the city and county agencies that provide service and care for the indigent peoples in our city.
>
> In his typical exuberant fashion, David was off and running with the idea, when I stopped him, reminding him that this was not something we could pull off with our current staff. We had to find a qualified event coordinator to even consider the idea.
>
> Particularly as I have aged, despite the fact that I carry an iPhone, I occasionally double-book. On this particular day, I had scheduled two meetings with different men who barely knew each other on completely separate subjects, at the same time and place. When I arrived, they both looked expectantly at me, while I, completely embarrassed, acknowledged my failure. Since we were all there,

we met together. One of the brothers, the pastor of a Charismatic congregation, was discussing a church discipline problem he was facing, while the other, an elder at a Bible congregation, spoke about fund-raising strategies.

During the course of the conversation, I mentioned David's idea for the special event and asked if either of them knew a good conference coordinator. Simultaneously, they both responded, "Janie Fountain." I had never heard of her and was amazed that two men from such separate backgrounds would know her and simultaneously, enthusiastically recommend her to me. I knew God was up to something, so I set an appointment with Janie, and the two of us then met with David Dalgleish. We all hit it off immediately, and she organized and successfully led our first In The City For the City event at the Bob Bullock Museum.

What Dan thought was a mistake in double booking, was God's way of bringing a woman of peace to the transformation blueprint. Janie turned out to be much more than an event planner. She soon joined the ABBA staff as the Assistant Executive Director. She had fostered deep relationships in the prayer movement and had carried a vision of the whole city covered with prayer for some time. She also had a prophetic type gifting to see, understand, and connect the pieces in a unique way. She saw the In the City for the City event this way:

The title, In the City for the City, envisioned what we felt like God wanted to do as a movement. It wasn't a program. It wasn't anything that was thought up by man. It was birthed through David Dalgleish and Dan Davis. We felt God wanted to unite the Body of Christ—not just churches, but ministries and non-profits and government agencies, as well as churches. He wanted them to move together as one for the city.

It was a large event and a prestigious location. Whether or not Bob Bullock knew it, he had caught a glimpse of God's vision. That vision was every man woman and child, every person from every walk of life, rich/poor, righteous/sinner, everyone coming together to make Texas what it was meant to be. When you enter the Bob Bullock museum—when you first walk in—you see this mural on the floor. It's a picture of the vision Bob Bullock had for Texas. It has Indians, Caucasians, and Asians. It has adults and children—people from every walk of life. It takes everyone coming together and working together to do what God wants to do. So it was very fitting and very much the plan of God that we had the event in that place. The Body of Christ in Austin had never had an event of that magnitude in such a prestigious place.

At that time in the city, the Spirit of God had been hindered by our lack of unity. People were doing the same work and had the same vision and didn't even know each other. Resources were limited, whereas together they were abundant. People were limited, whereas together there were more than enough. I felt like the main thing accomplished was to bring the Body of Christ together. The movement of God before was at an okay pace, but I felt it wasn't going to be good enough for the future. I felt the Lord took the Body of Christ, put us together in a slingshot, and shot us forward at an entirely different pace. Things we had prayed for years began to happen.

I will never forget the joy of the Lord in that place. It was electric when you walked in the museum. I felt the Lord was so thrilled in bringing His family together. It was like a family reunion. It was such a joy for me to walk around all the booths and see everyone talking together. That night nobody cared what church you went to. It was just family togetherness.

Janie brought her piece of vision into ABBA for four years. She put together two In the City for the City events, brought in an entirely different level of prayer, and changed ABBA with her prophetic insight. Then the Lord called her to San Francisco. When she left ABBA, Alan told the staff, "We aren't going to replace Janie. We are going to see how the Lord reshapes us to fit the gifts and vision of the people He's given us."

Reshaping to fit the people the Lord gives us—that's the principle of the man of peace. Consider the ones God brings. Discover the vision God has placed in their hearts. See how it fits with the larger vision. When the time for their vision is completed, allow God to move them to their next assignment and seek God for what He's doing now. Who carries the next piece? The In the City for the City piece took an interesting turn.

The Pastors' Strategic Council

The dream for the In the City for the City event began to take shape in 2007. The first event was held in the fall of 2008, and the last one was November 15, 2009. During that time frame another significant vision was taking form. This time Tim Hawks was the man of peace who connected with Dan Davis.

In the last chapter we saw how pastors began to see they needed to work together. Through Pastors in Covenant (PIC) groups, relationships and trust had been growing among pastors. Hurricane Katrina proved to be the catalyst of cooperation to show them it would take a united effort to impact the city. The In City for the City event brought another picture of what could happen if the city joined forces.

Through their experience with Katrina, pastors began to say, "We really can do something together." Tim Hawks already carried a burden for what the "something" needed to be. He sat down with Dan Davis to discuss what it would look like to put together a council of pastors that would go beyond helping in social causes—and begin to target the lostness of the city.

They discussed the fact that, while the city has more churches per capita than most of the United States, Austin has more lost people now than they did twenty years ago. The city proper is becoming more unchurched every day—not so much in the suburbs, but downtown. They considered how to pull pastors together to talk about a more gospel-centered movement in the city. How could they work together as churches to begin to change the direction?

Then they made a list of ten pastors they felt had the same kind of heartbeat. They chose people they had known from covenant groups and other meetings. In March of 2009, they invited those ten pastors to come to a meeting at Gateway Church. Not really having any idea why they were there, they came.

Dan and Tim raised a question, "If God, whenever He moves, always raises up leaders, then who are the leaders that God's raising up for His movement in this city? If not us, then who? And if not now, when?"

In that conversation there wasn't anybody sitting around that table saying, "Oh, man, I have an answer for the city. I know how to do this." There was a lot of trepidation and a lot of questions like: "Who are we to speak to the other churches in Austin and propose a direction?" But everybody came away with the sense that we're gaining favor and losing ground. We're gaining favor with the community, but when it comes to actual numbers of people going to heaven, we're losing ground. Dan and Tim challenged the pastors to consider three things: Would you be willing to tithe your time to the city? Would you be willing to pray together about what God might want to do? Would you be willing to get away together for two days?

The answer was yes, they would. In May 2009 the pastors gathered again for a 24-hour retreat to seek God for His heart for the city. Rob Harrell, First Evangelical Free Church, asked the group, "If Jesus were to walk into this room and say to us, 'This is what I want you guys to do—this is what I want your churches and the other churches of Austin to join you in,' what would He say to us?" After spending time praying, listening, and sharing what Rob called "sanctified thinking" together, they had a list of 46 impressions of what God might be saying to them. That night Dan and Tim took the list to see if there were themes. The next day they looked at what it would mean to own the lostness of the city. They proposed a framework to move forward, including a commitment of time and of meeting regularly to pray, talk and form strategy. Rob explained, "What really stokes the fires is that we really believe God wants us to do this. It's about dreaming things that have never been dreamed before. It's not about trying to obligate God to fulfill our plans. We really want to know what He wants us to do." Thus the Pastors' Strategic Council was born.

Greater Impact for Greater Austin

One of the first efforts of the Pastors' Strategic Council was to hire Ed Stetzer, a missiologist with LifeWay Research, to conduct a survey of local pastors plus 1,200 randomly selected residents of the community to gather information on the spiritual state of Austin. Then they hosted an event called "Greater Impact for Greater Austin," where more than 200 pastors gathered at Grace Covenant Church to hear Stetzer present the results of his survey. He closed with, "The normal Christian life is lived on mission. People (in Austin) aren't on mission, because they think their mission is coming to church. We need to change the ethos in our churches to be a people on mission, not a people who attend an experience. Churches need to look more like a team sport and less like a theatrical presentation."

Will Davis, pastor of Austin Christian Fellowship, challenged his fellow pastors to view church differently. "God sees the different pastors of the city as co-pastors of just one church. I'd like you to change your mindset. Consider yourself *a* pastor of *the* church, not *the* pastor of *a* church."

The pastors watched ten men—some Charismatic, some Evangelical, some denominational, some African-American, some Anglo—ten very different men, representing a wide cross-section of the city, joke about their differences and speak passionately about their common mission. The evening closed with pastors praying for one another around the altar. The event put more cracks in the limited mindsets and spiritual barriers.

In the City for the City—deeper and higher

By the second Greater Impact event on November 11, 2010, the Pastors' Strategic Council had found a way to brand the movement. Appropriately, they called it "In the City for the City." What Janie Fountain had referred to as a movement at the Bob Bullock Texas History Museum, had become one.

One piece of the emerging vision was to expose and tear down the walls of pride, prejudice, and preservation that have separated and weakened Christ's Body for centuries. A suggested way of doing that was to plan a "Walls Campaign" for the next fall where pastors all over the city would expose the walls through sermons and activities, and adopt a common theme—"In the City, for the City." The purpose would be to minimize differences and maximize impact for the greater good of God's purposes in central Texas. The Walls Campaign was a vision that grew out of the heart of Ryan Rush, pastor of Bannockburn Baptist Church and a member of the Pastors' Strategic Council.

Another piece of the movement, which congregations could take part in, was an adopt-a-school mentoring program. The Pastors' Strategic Council, while working on strategy, had met with the superintendents of five area school districts and asked to identify their greatest educational needs. Of the four major needs presented, the pastors especially picked up on this one: If a child can't read by the time he or she finishes third grade, the chances of graduating from high school are almost nonexistent, and without that diploma the chances of that child ending up on welfare rolls and even in jail are exponentially increased. So the pastors proposed that churches work together to adopt their area schools, or partner with a church across town to impact a school with great need. A special thrust would be to provide enough mentors to see to it that every third grader could read.

Step by step the Pastors' Strategic Council has moved forward in practical ways to fulfill the mission to "connect the church and its resources so that every man, woman, and child can see and hear the compelling mission of Christ's love for them."

The ebb and flow of the man of peace

The River of God flows through our city. The Lord wants a people who care about and care for the city they live in. He put the vision in the heart of Dan Davis, a pastor, to unite pastors. Pastors in Covenant groups grew out of his heart and flowed through the city, producing the fruit of relationship. God lit a vision in the heart of David Dalgleish, a businessman, for an event that involved ministries and pastors and city services uniting to get a picture of what they could do together. He named it In the City for the City. God joined what He had fostered in Janie Fountain to the flow. He took a minister, Tim Hawks, with an apostolic gift and vision, to draw together pastors and encourage them to bring their own gifts. Ryan Rush offered God-given insight on tearing down walls. Larry Coulter, Shepherd of the Hills Presbyterian Church, added his passion for education. John Burke, Gateway Church, brought his love and compassion for the lost, and on and on. These, and many others, are all men and women of peace whose passion has grown for the city from within the city.

In the midst of this, He added a man who was consciously looking for men and women of peace. God had sent Alan Nagel all over the world to give him a completely different perspective of a city. To him, Austin was more than home. It was a prototype—a laboratory to find out what it takes to transform a city. He had spent three years praying, meditating, and discussing principles with Campus Crusade. When he joined the ABBA team, he added that kind of big-picture thinking.

Finding the pieces to connect—relationships

Nagel says a big piece of building a movement is in finding God's pieces to connect. That can only be done through reality of relationship.

Some of the most promising leaders won't feel called to connect to your mission. Don't worry about that. Bless them to do what God has put in their hearts, and continue to build relationships all over the place to find the right ones. In His timing, God will bring along someone who doesn't seem very likely, who doesn't think like you do and won't do it like you would do it, and you will find in him or her, a missing piece. We must allow God to put His teams together His way. That will require getting to know one another's hearts to be able to see beyond your differences. It must build through authentic relationship.

Trust and relationship make up the glue that holds these pieces together. Relationships grow when God's people work shoulder to shoulder to build a common vision. As they push outside the narrow walls of their own church or ministry or community and discover that diversity gives a broader, more complete picture, amazing things happen. They find a bigger God, a bigger plan, and a more complete destiny. We have watched and experienced walls come down and transformation take place, as rich and rewarding relationships put steel in the structure.

The men and women of peace who carry vision necessary to transform a city are found through relationship, nurtured through relationship, and welded together into God's city-transforming army through relationship. It's one body under one head. It's a process, but with God, nothing is impossible.

Summary of principles
From Chapter 8:
- Transformation is birthed from a movement, not a ministry. It takes many ministries to make up a movement.

- A movement is Holy Spirit led. Ministries can be built on man's ideas, but apart from the direction and anointing of the Holy Spirit, the best man can produce is fairly effective programs. Programs won't transform anything. Only God can do that.
- Transformation moves out of clear God-given vision and mission.

From this chapter:

- Find the men and women of peace. Jesus' directive in Luke 10 is to look for the "man of peace." Men and women of peace carry part of God's vision that burns within. It's something God has planted in their hearts that they are called to do. They are the ones who will take hold of a task and do it in God's strength and anointing, because it's God-assigned, not man-driven. This principle is the opposite of pressuring people to join your program. Rather, it is discovering the gift within them and helping them find their place to release it.
- Everything is built on relationship. Individuals and organizations are not numbers to be manipulated toward some end. They carry treasure and purpose from the Lord to be respected and honored. Seldom is treasure lying around on the surface where you can easily see it. Treasure requires time and genuine relationship to uncover.

Questions to consider:

1. Are you a "man or woman of peace" for your city? What is the vision in your heart that won't go away?

2. Can you identify some men and women of peace in your city? In your neighborhood?

3. What aspects of your community promote relationship across denominational, cultural, and spatial boundaries?

4. If Jesus were to walk into this room and say to us, "This is what I want you guys to do—this is what I want your churches and the other churches of Austin to join you in," what would He say to us? Consider that question for your city.

Chapter 11

LOVE YOUR NEIGHBOR

The concept of people helping people is nothing new. That idea trails back through "Love your neighbor as yourself" and through Joseph setting up storehouses in Egypt, to a man called Abraham, through whom God promised to bless all peoples. On the back roads of organized goodness, you will usually find a man or woman with a God-given vision that won't turn loose of his or her heart.

In 2009, representatives from almost 150 ministries and non-profits filled the Bob Bullock Texas State History Museum for the second In the City for the City event. They were typical of hundreds of other such groups in Central Texas that work to meet the needs of the poor, the hurting, the helpless, the undereducated, and on and on. Every such ministry has a special story. Since I can't tell all their stories, I have chosen a few that portray principles essential to transforming a city. Please understand that the individuals whose names appear here are only the face of what took place through their ministries. They carried the vision, but they would be the first to tell you that only the Lord and an army of volunteers made their work successful.

Father Richard McCabe—eyes to see, ears to hear, hearts to respond

Our first "love story" started in 1958 when a Roman Catholic priest, Richard McCabe, started commuting from Austin, where he was an assistant pastor, to Lakeway, where he began holding mass in people's homes. Both Catholics and Protestants were hungry for spiritual guidance in Lakeway, so Father McCabe helped found the Lakeway Ecumenical Church, which served both Catholics and Protestants until it split in the mid-nineties.[1] This uniquely ecumenical attitude is a clear picture of the heart of the man who founded many other things in the Austin area. "If it was a cause that had a social definition, it mattered to Father McCabe," said McCabe's longtime friend Reverend Tom Carroll. "Whether it was helping abused women, or clothing and feeding the poor, you could be certain Father McCabe was behind it somewhere."[2]

Father McCabe was behind the founding of two more Catholic churches, two Catholic schools, and Big Brothers of Austin. "A Certified Social Worker and Certified Chemical Dependency Specialist, he built or acquired thousands of units for low-income housing in Austin and Central Texas and established hundreds of beds at treatment centers assisting adolescent and adult addicts and alcoholics. He was instrumental in the founding of numerous St. Vincent de Paul organizations and thrift shops for the needy. In the sixties he orchestrated the Caritas Refugee Services, benefiting thousands of homeless Asian, European, and Cuban refugees."[3]

Father McCabe founded Caritas (the name means charity) in 1964 to help connect people experiencing poverty and homelessness with public assistance. From an organization with a $30,000 budget, supported that first year by the Catholic Diocese of Austin, Caritas has grown (by 2012) to become a private nonprofit with a 7.7 million dollar budget.[4] "Caritas is the largest source of non-governmental assistance (not a government agency, but about 60 percent governmental dollars) for low-income families in Travis County and serves the working poor, the unemployed, the homeless, the near-homeless, and documented refugees. Caritas offers education classes on practical topics to build life skills such as budgeting, money management, energy conservation, ESL (English as a second language), and job readiness and placement."[5]

One man, who was able to hear the cries for help and to see the potential for good in the people around him, had the unique capacity to connect the potential to the need. Father McCabe didn't provide the money to build schools and churches. He didn't provide the manpower to help the helpless. He provided the heart that God could use as a catalyst to pull a community together. *A first ingredient for building a ministry is a man or woman with a God-inspired vision, who is willing to hear, to see, and to respond.*

Lori DeVillez—life, prayer, provision, and the power of unity

The next story centers on a woman with a God-inspired, God-driven vision. Lori DeVillez, founder of Austin Pregnancy Resource Center, has the audacity to believe that where God gives vision, He is also responsible to open the way and make provision.

Lori's passion is life—saving the lives of unborn babies and leading people to eternal life in Christ. Shortly after she graduated from college, she knew she was called to missions, but mission trips overseas did not seem to be her calling. Lori recalled:

> Our church gave us a spiritual gift inventory and told us to sign up with the ministry that matched our gifts. The pregnancy center that our church helped support matched my gifts of evangelism and administration.
>
> The first day I reported to the center, there was a girl waiting at the door. I asked her if she was the volunteer for the day. She said, "No, I'm here for a pregnancy test." I'd never run a pregnancy test. I didn't know what I was doing, but my degree was psychology, and we were trained to never let them see you sweat. Always stay calm. So I figured it out, and we got through that day. Her test was negative. I knew how to share the gospel, and she accepted Christ that day. I got so excited. I knew this was my mission field!

For Lori, the hub of God's chosen mission field is Austin, Texas. When she moved to Austin in 1997, her first question was: "Where's the pregnancy center by the UT campus? Fifty thousand students, five abortion facilities (at that time), and one Life Care tucked away on Anderson Lane—I thought, 'Why isn't there a pregnancy center by the campus?' Everybody told me, "You'll never get by UT." Nobody was even willing to try."

Lori prayed and talked to pastors. Finally, when she shared her vision with Pastor Michael Lewis of Great Hills Baptist Church, he asked, "How much would it cost?" She told him, and he said, "Let's do it, and I'll help you raise the money." He called Pastor Ryan Rush of Bannockburn Baptist, and they called other pastors. Lori told the story:

> We held our first meeting at Great Hills in October, 2004, to start Austin Pregnancy Resource Center. Ninety-one people came. I said that night (I always do), if a group's ready to start a center, set an opening date, so you have a target to work toward. We set the date for January 16, 2005, because January is Sanctity of Life month. Pastor Lewis called it the building of the Nehemiah Wall. We tore down the walls of Jericho, and we built a Nehemiah Wall, because within 52 days we were open, even despite the holidays. It was full speed then, but it had taken seven years of prayer.
>
> When people around the country say, "How did you get by a major university? No pregnancy center's ever gotten by a major university," my answer is prayer. *The source of any action is prayer. Prayer is what it takes.* Let God open the doors.
>
> When we had our lease and moved into this facility, I said we needed to purchase the property. Shortly afterwards, the sorority next door decided they wanted to buy our building. They contacted the

owner, who teaches at UT. According to our lease, they only had to give me a 30-day notice. So he called to give the notice. I said, "Well, Dr. Walton, you know I want to buy." He said, "What collateral do you have?" Because we were a new nonprofit, I said, "We have a sonogram machine." He started laughing. "Do you know their building's free and clear at $2,000,000?" I said, "So?" He said, "I tell you what. If you can raise $30,000 in 30 days, I'll sell it to you." We did it in two weeks, so he sold to us, owner-financed."

Austin Pregnancy Resource Center (APRC) runs on God's economy. Lori says, "When you know it's God, and when you know how He works and the power of prayer, and you're part of just flowing with the Body, there's no limit to what He can do." Since APRC opened in 2005, Lori's team has helped open twelve more independent pregnancy resource centers in the area. When Lori first came to town in 1997, she started praying with a friend at the Capitol every Monday from 12:00 to 12:30. They'd pray, "Lord, would you change the laws of this state?" Ten years they prayed, asking God to change the laws, asking God to raise up godly leaders, asking God to build a culture of life, every Monday praying for that.

There had been no laws in the state favoring life since 1986. The next session (1997–99) three bills passed. Since that time, a succession of pro-life bills have passed, including Woman's Right to Know, Parental Consent of Minor, and the Sonogram Law, which is the strongest in the nation.

Facilities and laws are only part of God's overarching plan for life. Lori believed that God wanted coalition. Shortly after moving into the Austin Pregnancy Resource Center, Lori began a coalition called Austin Area Life Affirming Coalition (AALAC).

When I started the coalition eight years ago, I just wanted to break down the walls of territory and competitiveness, so I formed the coalition for that purpose. That has been accomplished. Now AALAC encompasses pregnancy centers, maternity homes, adoption agencies, abstinence groups, after care, anyone interested in health care, and people from Superior Health and Medicaid. Fifty organizations, including St. David's Hospital, form AALAC.

Many are coming, because they are finding that the pregnancy centers are now the ones with the resources. With all the changes in the government budgets—cuts and limitations—we're the ones where there's no red tape. There's no tie-up. We can refer—just like CPS (Child Protective Services)—they call here all the time, and we're able to help them with diapers and formula, and we're connecting with their clients. They're not sharing the Gospel, but we can. So it's opening all kinds of new doors to present the Gospel.

That's the reason Lori has never received money from the government. At one point there was $5,000,000 available for pregnancy centers. Lori wasn't interested. "If you remove the prayer and the Gospel, you miss the mission. That's why I'll never be interested in government money. The mission, of course, is saving lives. The baby doesn't choose abortion. The mom does or the boyfriend does or the grandma does. If we don't reach the hearts of the family, what's that baby going to grow up in anyway? That's what I'm about—sharing the Gospel. That's where the power is."

Non-Christian groups are welcome as part of the coalition, but it is run by Christian principles. Fifty organizations combining forces get a lot more done. They refer clients to one another, providing a much broader coverage to help people with needs. They also form a powerful base of legislative information and testimony. "When the pro-life legislators needs testimony for different bills that are up, they send out one email—"here's what it is, here's what we need," and we can get clients there that have strong testimony. It helps in getting life-supporting laws."

In the 1960's, right here in Austin, seeds were sown that led to the monumental Roe v. Wade Supreme Court decision that pronounced a death sentence to millions of unborn babies.[6] As He so often does, God chose the place where offense started to launch a counter attack. He found a young woman in Indiana with a passion for life and transplanted her into the heart of Texas, where *she used the keys of prayer, obedience, trusting God for provision, and building coalition through relationship* to replace a culture of death with a movement for life.[7]

Chris Rowley–coalition for neighborhood transformation

Chris Rowley has worked closely with Lori DeVillez since Lori moved to Austin. Indeed, Chris was the prayer partner who went with Lori weekly to pray for life issues at the Texas State Capitol, but the Lord took Chris' ministry in a different direction. He gave her the desire to educate women and help them find confidence and employment. She has been the face of the Christian Women's Job Corps (CWJC) in Austin for around twenty years. CWJC helps women earn a GED, giving them the equivalent of a high school diploma, and learn both job skills and life skills within a Christian context. As the needs of the community became clearer, other ministries and services—such as Simple Church in apartment complexes and teaching English as a second language—developed and served the community in tandem with CWJC. They joined under the title of River City Hope Street, still under Chris' leadership. Recently, River City Hope Street has joined forces with several ministries and churches that serve the same group of people in East Austin. They have formed a coalition called Servants of the City. Chris describes the coalition this way:

> Ministries, nonprofits, and churches, which have a burden for a particular people group or segment of the community, form little partnerships. For example, Mission Possible, River City Hope Street, Austin Pregnancy Resource Center, Greater Mount Zion Baptist Church, and some other churches are working together closely to reach the same

people. We provide more than a resource list. We have food, clothes, education, and pregnancy resources—all at the Mission Possible facility. We provide children's ministry with Big Fish, apartment ministry through Hope Street, and summer camps for the kids. There is a medical facility right here in the Mission Possible facility for people we are all ministering to. We're all ministering to the same people, providing for different needs, but working closely together.

What usually happens with a family in need—they'll go to one service provider, who will help them in one area and might give them a resource name or tell them to call 2-1-1 to get help in other areas, and it seldom happens. We're using Charity Tracker[8], so the Martinez family (hypothetical family) comes to Christian Men's Job Corp, and we help dad get his GED. We find they have a pregnant teenager, so we send a referral for them to the Pregnancy Resource Center. Everybody in the Charity Tracker Network has access to what we've put in the database for the Martinez family. When they look them up in Charity Tracker, they see dad's working on his GED, mom's taking a sewing class, teenager needs help because she's pregnant, they got food from the Mission Possible food pantry, and Greater Mount Zion helped them with their rent. Everybody in the network can see the help given to the Martinez family. There's accountability, so it provides a safety net for the service providers as well. We can walk the Martinez family through this crisis to helping them meet their own needs. We are actively partnering together to help families.

The ministries that make up this particular team have long-standing relationships. They've grown up together, partnering in many ways over the years. *They have learned that they are much more effective working together than each trying to meet the community's needs independently. In coalition they make a bigger dent on the needs of the area.*

Daniel Geraci—trust and obey

Daniel Geraci is gifted with a simple, old-fashioned faith—if God says it, you do it. For Daniel, God's first call was an attention-getter: "I had a vision from the Lord about a house. In 1997, before I was even a believer, I was in a restaurant with a friend, and we were just talking about cars and boats and secular stuff. Suddenly, out of nowhere, our conversation changed, and the Holy Spirit descended upon us. We had this vision. We could both see it. We saw a house where people came from all over the city to reach out to the poor and needy of the city. I called it a house of unity. We left the restaurant saying, 'What just happened to us.' We didn't know the Holy Spirit, so we tried to manufacture what we'd seen. We gathered a bunch of unbelievers and started buying sandwiches and trying to feed the poor. It all fell apart. I believe what the Lord has me doing now is part of this 'house of unity vision for our city.'"

Daniel is now the Executive Director and Founder for the Austin Disaster Relief Network (ADRN). After that initial vision and the failed attempt to do God's thing through man's ability, Daniel came to know the Lord in a personal way and became a leader in the prayer movement. You will remember part of his story from Chapter 7. He built many solid relationships with pastors and prayer leaders as he simply kept doing the next thing he sensed God saying.

In September 2005, Hurricane Katrina devastated New Orleans, causing over 6,200 families to be evacuated into the Austin Convention Center. The scene was chaotic. Hundreds of local pastors tried their best to access and penetrate the convention center to help those in need. However, due to a lack of training and the mistakes of a few pastors, the majority of pastors were turned away.

Because of the large evacuation of families into the greater Austin area, Daniel took the month of September off from work. "Many of the New Orleans families wanted to be sponsored by churches in the community. My wife and I sponsored two families and brought them into our own home to meet their immediate needs. During this time, I was on the phone with Pastor Chad Patterson, then associate pastor of Church of the Hills. We were discussing the devastation of the people affected by Katrina, when suddenly I had a vision. I saw a network of churches, ministries, and businesses within our city, working together to sponsor and meet the needs of every family affected by disaster. I also saw our city divided into 12 sectors, with a sector leader over every sector to help coordinate disaster relief efforts. Within every church on the network, there was a disaster relief coordinator that would help coordinate the disaster relief efforts effectively within their church. The entire vision would ultimately bring a well-coordinated response from a well-trained church in our city to meet the emotional, spiritual and physical needs of those affected by disaster. I wrote the whole vision on a napkin."

So the vision for ADRN (Austin Disaster Relief Network) came at the time of Katrina, but didn't become reality until three hurricanes later. Hurricane Ike had brought the last of some 44,000 refugees to Austin in two years. The city resources were overwhelmed, pastors were frustrated, because they couldn't get into shelters to minister to the hurting people, and the time was ripe for an organized approach to disaster relief.

Daniel said:

> I believe the biggest factor that caused pastors to be open to the idea of ADRN was due to their frustration and inability to truly impact the lives of the 44,000 evacuees that flooded into our city since 2005. The importance of a unified body, training, and coordinated relief could no longer be overlooked.

In February 2009, we sat before the Assistant Director with the City of Austin Office of Homeland Security and Emergency Management and a Red Cross representative and asked, "How can we serve you?" They said we were the first representatives from the church community that had ever asked them this question. They came up with 5 needs to meet:

1. Help them find and train shelter managers
2. Help them find and train shelter volunteers
3. Financially adopt shelters to meet the small needs of families, such as hearing aid batteries, pillows, bus tickets, etc.
4. Help them find churches that will become intermediate shelters
5. Adopt families affected by disaster, short and long-term

In March 2009, with lots of prayer and no money, ADRN became the official disaster relief network for the churches of Greater Austin. Within the first year, approximately eight hundred Christian volunteers were trained by Red Cross standards in shelter operations. ADRN also set up an Emergency Broadcast System (mass email, text, and voice messaging) to reach and deploy volunteers within a minute's notice and a Mobile Emergency Call Center, to act as a central command post for the Body of Christ to communicate with each other, marshal resources and receive calls from those affected by disaster. By June 2010, ADRN began offering Critical Incident Stress Management (CISM) training, which is an internationally recognized program for trauma debriefing, and Community Emergency Response Team (CERT) training, which is a certified training to help volunteers know how to respond to a disaster within their community and work along-side of first responders.

In 2011 ADRN teams dealt with a flood in Williamson County and fires in Oak Hill and Leander. Then came the Bastrop fire. Daniel tells the story:

When the fires began, we set up our command center at Hill Country Bible Church. The call center received five hundred to a thousand calls a day for those first five to seven days. We had over forty people around the clock answering calls and doing administrative work. Survivors were calling into our call center to have their needs met and our volunteers would end most calls in prayer. We had stepped out in faith and done what the Lord had told us to do, and He always does His part.

I was with a staff member for the Bastrop Sherriff's Department when they received a call that said the state Critical Incident Stress Management (CISM) team, which was supposed to be deployed to do all the debriefing, was sent to another city. The Sheriff's staffer looked at me and asked if ADRN could provide enough volunteers trained in CISM to help debrief families affected by the disaster. In faith, I told them "yes" and that I had over four hundred trained CISM volunteers to reach out to for the assignment. So because of this God moment, ADRN was chosen to lead in the deployment with a police escort into the neighborhoods, prior to any survivors going back to their home. On the first day, ADRN deployed over one hundred CISM trained volunteers. By the fifth day, we had over a hundred twenty-five pastors and three hundred CISM trained volunteers deployed to meet the emotional and spiritual needs of those affected by the disaster. Once in the field, our teams would find themselves loving and embracing survivors as they saw what remained of their homes for the first time. Many had to bury the owner's cats and dogs. Survivors received comfort and much prayer as teams invited God into their situations. Our CISM team debriefed an estimated 1,400 survivors. All were asked if they wanted a church from our network to sponsor and walk with them through the rebuilding process. Over 525 families said yes.

I found out months later, at a Bastrop Ministerial Alliance meeting with seventeen pastors present, that a revival had broken out in Bastrop! Survivors were turning back to God, and church leaders were noticing a change in hearts of their people and new converts. The impact of churches sponsoring hundreds of families was revealing the goodness of God and causing hearts to turn and seek His face.

Bastrop was a training ground for what was to come. On April 17, 2013, a massive explosion at the West Fertilizer Company storage and distribution facility wreaked havoc and destruction in West, Texas. Over 150 homes were destroyed and several more severely damaged. On April 18, ADRN deployed teams to West to help with the aftermath of the disaster. This time ADRN provided, not only feet on the ground, but also organizational guidance and training to West and Waco, which formed their own Disaster Relief Network to adopt the families left homeless by the explosion. The newly formed Waco Disaster Relief Network sponsored approximately 283 families.

It seemed the dust had barely settled in West when, on May 20, a deadly tornado hit Moore, Oklahoma, destroying over 1,200 homes. Again ADRN teams were deployed. Again they served, ministered God's love and miracles, and again they provided the leadership and know-how to organize churches in the Oklahoma City area to start their own Disaster Relief Network.

A vision from God, scribbled on a napkin, has become a powerful, unified thrust from Central Texas that is bringing hope, help, and multiplication to other parts of the nation. Daniel is living proof that a man, who simply listens to and obeys God, can build something out of nothing. It hasn't been easy. Along with the many volunteers who have received training, Daniel also gives a lot of credit to the prayer team that is also on duty every time the feet on the ground go out to serve. Feet on the ground need support from the heavens. With that combination, they've seen many miracles.

Love wears many faces. When it comes to meeting the needs of those who are hurting and in trouble, the possible activities are limitless, but the principles seem to be consistent. This list is not exhaustive, but it includes:

1. Vision—a man or woman with a God-given vision.
2. Prayer—before, during, and ongoing—is essential to hear God's direction, to walk in His ways, and to keep His perspective in the midst of every circumstance.
3. Faith—ministries that go beyond the ability of human resources must understand and trust the character and ability of the One whose resources are unlimited.
4. Relationship—most ministries are built on a volunteer base. The trust, value, and mutual honor that make such things work come out of genuine relationship.
5. Coalition—to transform a city, ministries must move from a silo mentality to an understanding of what Paul was talking about in Ephesians 4:16: *He makes the whole body fit together perfectly. As each part does its own special work, it helps the other parts grow, so that the whole body is healthy and growing and full of love. (NLT)* (Silos are ministries that do their own thing in their own locality, but have not learned to connect with other ministries to meet broader needs more efficiently.)

Questions to consider:
1. What person(s) in your city carries a vision that won't let go of him or her? What has God already done with the vision? Where do you see it going?

2. Where is relationship between ministries being built? Where could such relationship be built? What ministries are working on a related issue (like the life issue)? What

ministries are working to help the same people group? How could they do it better together?

3. What would it take in your neighborhood or your city to get people to come together to begin forming relationship?

END NOTES

1. "Community mourns the loss of Monsignor Richard McCabe"
Monday, September 14, 2009 | *Smithville Times* |
2. Ibid.
3. From Father McCabe's obituary in the *Austin American Statesman* http://www.legacy.com/obit-uaries/statesman/obituary.aspx?n=richard-e-mc-cabe&pid=132864302#fbLoggedOut
4. http://www.caritasofaustin.org/index.php/about/history
5. http://austintex.com/caritas-austin-food-pantry-soup-kitchen-free-meals-life-skills
6. http://www.tshaonline.org/handbook/online/articles/jrr02
7. Many people have poured out their lives in the life movement here in Austin, such as Elizabeth McClung with Coalition for Life. I deeply regret not being able to give credit where credit is due. In each section of this chapter, I have had to settle for sharing the story of an individual whose life clearly illustrates keys to transformation that might be useful in other places.
8. A web application for shared case management

Chapter 12

GOD'S TAPESTRY

2013—a year of shift

The Pastors' Strategic Council started the year with a big vision, or perhaps I should say they joined Dan Smith's big vision. Dan Smith is a tech guy who wanted to use his skill and his money to encourage people to talk about God and about life's hard questions—not just church people, not even just Christians. Dan wanted to include everyone in the conversation, so he created a website, exploregod.com, to encourage people to interact around spiritual questions. The Pastors' Strategic Council agreed to join Dan's project by enabling him to use Austin as his test city, so the Explore God campaign has woven its way into the fiber of 2013 like an accent color in a tapestry.

The Hand weaving the tapestry used His colors in ways no one expected or could have predicted. The first touch was on March 27, 2013. The American Atheist Association decided to celebrate its 50th anniversary by returning to the city where it all started—Austin, Texas. The Pastors' Strategic Council decided to use the opportunity to set the tone for Explore God by engaging unbelievers in an authentic, humble, spiritual conversation. They invited the leaders of the American Atheist Association to join them for a friendly discussion to promote understanding. The pastors proved to be cordial hosts, answering questions honestly and with genuine respect and kindness. After it was over, one of the atheists expressed her surprise that Christians could be so nice.

What else happened that night? Gail Long, leader of Freedom's Fire, a national prophetic team, saw it this way: "I knew the discussion with the atheists was an initial prophetic act to declare a shift in the church in this region—that we were going to stand up, talk about our differences, humbly in a godly way, but freely in a public forum. No more hiding, no more we-don't-know-what-to-do-with-the-atheists, we-don't-know-what-to-do-with-the-homosexuals, or we-don't-know-what-to-do-with-the-drug-culture. There's this rising up." It felt like the people of God stepped through a door into a new freedom to truly be the people of God.

There was another interesting thing about the timing of this event. The Lord still seems to like the Hebrew calendar. It's interesting that March 27, 2013, was the 16th of Nisan on the Hebrew Calendar. Nisan 16 is the second day of Passover. It celebrates the Israelites' departure from Egypt. Egypt stands for bondage and slavery to sin and the world system. Is it possible that while the atheists celebrated fifty years as an organization, God lifted off His church in Austin the painful burden of having allowed atheism a door into the nation through our city? And what tools did He use to bring freedom? He used what He always uses—love, humility, and kindness. God doesn't like the spiritual forces that blind people to the truth, but He deeply loves the people.

The conflict of kingdoms at the state capitol

As far as I know, the next strands woven into the 2013 tapestry were not related to the Explore God campaign, but on second thought, perhaps they were. The churches had used the early summer months to train their people to engage folks in spiritual conversations. Part of the training was to view people as God's masterpieces, even if they were covered with the mud of sin. It also had to do with representing the loving character and nature of God. That training, which took place in a couple hundred churches, might have affected people's attitudes in what happened next, but my sense at the time was that the Holy Spirit did a sovereign work.

On June 25, the Texas Senate was set to vote on one of the most stringent abortion bills in the nation. The House had already passed the bill. On the last day of the special session, Senator Wendy Davis staged an eleven-hour filibuster in hopes that time would run out before the vote could be taken. The filibuster was broken on technicalities, but a raucous crowd succeeded in preventing the vote until time had expired. The bill died amid a near riot of jeering protesters.

On June 26, Governor Rick Perry called a second special session to address the issue, and God called out His people. The Texas Capitol became the staging ground of a graphic spiritual battle. People in orange shirts came from across the nation to do everything in their power to block the bill. They staged sit-ins in the rotunda, chained themselves to the rails in the gallery, shouted and cursed to disrupt testimony and proceedings. They mocked God and did their best to intimidate both witnesses and legislators.

People dressed in blue came to pray, to testify, to affect the atmosphere with worship, and to fill space in the gallery to prevent screaming antagonists from disrupting the proceedings. Women who had suffered abortions lined up to testify to the pain and destruction that decision had caused in their lives. Many spoke of God's subsequent healing. Testimonies continued for hours, day after day. Women who had never talked about having had an abortion came forth to share their guilt and pain in front of television cameras as people jeered and tried to interrupt. They came from across the state, even the nation. Many said they showed up because they sensed God wanted them there.

Cindi Vana, Texas State Coordinator for the National Day of Prayer, was at the Capitol helping organize and direct prayer during much of the time. She described what she saw as the orchestration of the Lord. She said some people came with their own plans, but none of the man-made plans seemed to take hold. "God called people to come and gave them assignments for a day or days or hours, and they knew they'd been called up. It was by no means their effort. The Lord was saying the battle was His. We were just told to sit and watch and do exactly, specifically, what the Lord had shown each of us." The Lord called some to overcome their fear and testify. Others were directed to do spiritual warfare around the Capitol grounds. Others filled the gallery and prayed silently. Some wore red tape over their mouths, representing unborn babies who could not defend themselves. Cindi continued:

> The Lord was doing all kinds of things there. I asked, "What was it that shifted? What won the battle?" My sense is the victory was over the spirit of religion. It broke, because the people who came on the part of the church did not come with religious posters. They did not come to promote their religion or denomination or anything else. The religious spirit fell and what made it fall was the word of the testimony. Because there were not enough hours in the public area for testimony, they set up an area in the open rotunda for women or men to come and give their testimony. For nine hours each day for three days they told their stories. They were pushed. They were shoved. They were cursed. People were singing mocking words about Christianity and cursing Christ to the tune of "Amazing Grace." But the word of the testimony by women who said, "I had an abortion . . . I was lied to . . . I didn't know what it meant . . . I was held down . . . I suffered . . . Only God has healed me . . . The Lord has touched me . . . I took a life and God has touched me . . . Without God I couldn't have made it." Over and over again for twenty-seven hours women, along with men and even children, shared their testimonies. The testimony of God caused the strongholds to begin to shatter over the city.

Perhaps the most telling proof that the Lord was in charge was the common thread of patience and love exhibited by His people. In spite of cursing, shoving, and mocking, no one responded in kind. People who were there for hours, even days, said they could not remember anyone dressed in blue showing anger to the demonstrators. A number of people said they felt compassion for their adversaries. They were led to pray for the people, not just the circumstances. When interrupted by the abortion rights people at the pro-life rally, Lieutenant Governor David Dewhurst told them that they might not realize it, but, "We love you."

On July 13, 2013, the abortion bill passed the Texas Senate, and Governor Rick Perry signed it into law on July 18. Forty years earlier the Supreme Court decision of Roe v. Wade made abortion legal in the United States. An Austin lawyer, Sarah Weddington, had filed that case. The 2013 Texas law didn't eliminate what began here in 1973, nor did it bring back the lost babies, but it put some strong limitations on abortions in Texas. It was another shift that brought at least partial redemption for an old wrong, and it was done with tenacity, but in humility and love.

Explore God

In July billboards started popping up all over the Austin area encouraging people to Explore God. The billboards led to the Explore God website: www.exploregod.com. Signs appeared on churches inviting folks to join the conversation. The "conversation" was a sermon series plus small group discussions built around the seven most-asked spiritual questions according to Google—such things as "Does life have a purpose?" and "Why does God allow pain and suffering?"

The kickoff for the campaign was to be a citywide prayer and praise celebration, set for September 5. From the perspective of the leaders who were planning events, September 5 was a convenient date, after the Labor Day holiday but before the first sermon in the series. On God's calendar September 5, 2013 was Rosh Hashanah, the Jewish New Year—time for a new beginning. Among other things, Rosh Hashanah is a time of blowing the shofar and calling people to repentance. In Old Testament times, it was a call to preparation for the Feast of Tabernacles when the people built huts that represented God's presence dwelling among His redeemed people.[1]

While the pastors planned the prayer event, God gave David and Bethany Martin, leaders of the Heart of Texas House of Prayer (HOTHOP), another strand of the tapestry. The Martins were aware of the Hebrew calendar. They intentionally set aside forty days of 24/7 prayer and worship designed to end on September 5—Rosh Hashanah. They didn't know about the pastors' plans for the city celebration. Under God's orchestration, there were forty days of continual prayer and worship, which culminated on Rosh Hashanah with a sanctuary full of worshippers from all over the city, representing hundreds of churches, to dedicate and launch the Explore God campaign.

When the pastors started planning the Explore God campaign, they were praying for 100 congregations to participate. Instead, 377 churches took part. There were 1,500 small group discussions that took place in homes, in coffee shops, in restaurants—all sorts of places all over the area. From the reports that came in, many of those participants were not church members. Church attendance increased 10 percent in the area churches. The pastors believe they exceeded their goal of 400,000 spiritual conversations.

Beyond the numbers were the individual stories, like the man whose discussion group was held by Skype with his business associates from around the world. Thirty-four people came to Christ through the five discussion groups held within the Austin Police Department. The Round Rock churches joined forces to prayer walk all of Round Rock one Sunday evening before the Explore God kickoff. They met at designated places all over the city, gathering by neighborhood rather than by congregation. Prayer leaders from the churches and city intercessors met weekly from May through August and daily during the seven weeks of the campaign to cover the campaign in prayer. Prayer alliances were formed in various parts of the city. That's just a taste of what we know happened. Only God knows the whole story.

From individual to team to corporate, from gifts and callings and ministries to a body providing what every joint supplies (Ephesians 4:16), from pastor to teams to 377 churches joining in a unified thrust for the area—the tapestry slowly expands and takes shape. It includes a lot more people than anticipated. It includes the business community, the media, educators, government, and more. While the world system tries to build walls to shut the Lord out, the Master Weaver continues drawing hearts together through the threads of this great masterpiece.

This book features Austin, but God's story is much bigger than Austin. It's bigger than the church. It's bigger than any of our parts and pieces; nevertheless, our parts and pieces are important to the whole. People are flocking to Austin to be part of what is going on here, and Austin leaders are reaching out to discover and join forces with leaders from other cities who have their own God stories. As they share the pieces that God has given each one, tapestry joins to tapestry, and a kingdom picture emerges that is exceedingly abundantly above all that any of us imagined (Ephesians 3:20).

In the last chapter we will take a peek at what is happening from a variety of perspectives.

END NOTES
1. http://www.hebrew4christians.com/Holidays/Fall_ Holidays/Sukkot/sukkot.html

Chapter 13

PERSPECTIVE

Ephesians 4:11–16 And He Himself gave some to be apostles, some prophets, some evangelists, and some pastors and teachers, for the equipping of the saints for the work of ministry, for the edifying of the body of Christ . . . that we may grow up in all things into Him who is the head—Christ—from whom the whole body, joined and knit together by what every joint supplies, according to the effective working by which every part does its share, causes growth of the body for the edifying of itself in love. (NKJV)

As I have gathered information for this book, it has taken me on a journey in perspective. I've looked at the city through the eyes of African-American pastors and Hispanic pastors. I've seen it through the evangelistic mindset, focused intently on how to reach those who haven't met their Savior; and the ministry mindset, geared with equal passion toward meeting the physical and emotional needs of real people. I've experienced the hearts of worship leaders who have seen that the presence of God changes everything, and intercessors who understand that change takes place in the heavens before it can happen on earth. I've been touched by the deep passions of men and women who carry the burden of God for a particular aspect of His kingdom. Each one believes with all his or her heart that if the church would just get behind what God has given him or her to do, it would change the world. Who's right? I believe they all are. They each carry a unique reflection of the heart of Christ and of His multi-faceted kingdom. It takes all the parts to even begin to express God's character and His immense love.

Another thread that has been consistent through every aspect of this God journey is the march from individual to corporate: someone praying, to small groups praying, to prayer marches through the city; someone caring about the lives of unborn babies, to groups forming to provide help for unwed mothers, to a coordinated effort of over fifty ministries that support life throughout the region; pastors gathering in a small group for mutual support, to working together on city-wide initiatives, to strategizing together for ways to touch the whole city. There are those people who have been the forerunners and the spark plugs, followed by the organizers and relationship builders, followed by the strategists who see the big picture and understand how the pieces fit together.

In the ever-growing, ever-uniting, and ever-increasing plan of God, He is taking us from church to kingdom and from programs to principles to presence. Pastors in Austin are regularly reminded that they are not *the* pastor of *a* church; they are *a* pastor of *the* church. For pastors, the questions are becoming: Who are my sheep? Are they the people who gather within the walls on Sunday, or are they everyone in my geographic area? Is my job to care for the flock or to empower and send forth God's special forces? Who do I need to team up with to meet this kind of challenge?

Christ Together—the Pastors' Perspective

The Explore God Campaign gave area pastors fresh vision of what might be accomplished if they work together. The Pastors' Strategic Council used the momentum to introduce the next step, a movement called Christ Together. Christ Together is a growing, nationwide, city-reaching movement. Christ Together Greater

Austin expresses much of what the Pastors' Strategic Council has been developing over the past five years. Its mission: *To give every man, woman, and child in the Greater Austin area repeated opportunities to see, hear and respond to the gospel. Through every endeavor, plan, communication, and partnership, we will consistently and clearly demonstrate the life-changing reality of Jesus Christ.*[1]

It has four strategic areas of endeavor: spiritual awareness, acts of service, circles of accountability, and church planting. The Explore God Campaign was the 2013 thrust for "Spiritual Awareness." The results of that were reported in the last chapter.

For "Church Planting," the council has provided leadership and support for church planters. They provide equipping for church planters and an arena for planters to share plans, strategies, and best practices.

In the area called "Acts of Service," the Pastor's Strategic Council chose education as an area around which to unify the churches. After learning how critical it is for children to be able to read by the time they finish third grade, they decided to focus on addressing the problem of third grade literacy. Larry Coulter, pastor of Shepherd of the Hills Presbyterian Church, took the initiative on this point, and David Lloyd from the ABBA staff did the legwork on pairing churches with schools. With over 200 elementary schools located in Greater Austin, so far 90 churches have partnered with schools, providing one-on-one help for children while also lending support to the educators. Hundreds of literacy partners and mentors are already making a difference in the lives of students.[2]

The final strategic area is "Circles of Accountability," which refers to groups of pastors coming together in a specific geographic region to mobilize their congregations to reach every man, woman, and child in their circle of influence.[3] At this writing, eight regions have functioning circles, and several more are taking first steps.

The Pastors' Strategic Council provides a strong picture of the apostolic gift in action. They are results people. They are leaders. They pull together the pieces, put them in order, and get things done. They are providing the leadership for an evangelistic thrust to take the good news of Christ to the city. Their piece is crucial . .. but there are other crucial pieces as well.

What the Spirit is Saying—the Intercessors' Perspective

Sometimes the evangelistic apostles (apostles come in a variety of bents) and their followers are so focused on strategic organization of natural objectives that they fail to take into account the battle taking place in the spirit realm over the people they want to reach. It's okay if they don't focus there. That's not where their gifting lies. But we, and perhaps they, need to take in account the people God has gifted to see and understand that battle.

God gifted prophetic people with a greater awareness of what is taking place in the spirit realm. Often intercessors carry this type of anointing. Typically, prophetic intercessors don't fit very well in the local church. Because the gifting and call of an intercessor is so different from that of a pastor, it takes people capable of stepping beyond their calling to see God's bigger kingdom picture to enable a solid working relationship between the two. For those who can see the benefits of teaming anointings, it can be a powerful combination, especially if the pastor actually carries an apostolic gift. Then he or she can take the prophetic insight and gain a more complete perspective of how to fit the pieces together to overcome obstacles and achieve their goals.

In Austin, the intercessors have carried much of the spiritual battle for decades. They have prayer walked, prayed on-site in spiritually dark places, and declared and decreed the will of God over the city. (For more detail on the prayer movement, see Chapter 7.) They have also supported and given prayer coverage to events like March for Jesus and the yearly Pastors' Prayer Gathering. In the past few years several things have happened to build trust and a stronger working relationship between pastors and intercessors.

In 2009, God gave Trey Kent, pastor of Northwest Fellowship, the idea for Unceasing Prayer for the area.[4] He recruited churches to adopt one day a month and to organize their people to cover all twenty-four hours of their day in prayer. Since that time, there has always been someone praying, day and night, 24/7 for the city.

Trey has informally become known as the "prayer pastor" of the city. His passion for prayer is contagious.

In 2011, the ABBA prayer coordinators, Gail Long and Thana Rolph, asked for Trey's help to put together 40 Days of Prayer leading up to Palm Sunday. A wide variety of prayer and worship events filled the forty days. The period was kicked off by worship at Trey's church with Sean Feucht, the founder of The Burn, a group that leads intercessors and worshipers in extended periods of worship. That night proved to be the forerunner for what has turned into a worship explosion in the area.

Another result from that 40 Days of Prayer was the uniting of many of the city's prayer leaders to form Austin Kingdom Intercessors. They continue to meet monthly to seek a more unified prayer thrust for the area.

One small event during the 40 Days, called Encounter, was unique in that it intentionally went counter-culture to many traditions that divide the church. Encounter featured workshops led by both men and women, by three different ethnic groups, by seasoned teachers as well as young unknowns, by charismatics, evangelicals, and denominational people, and by both pastors and prayer leaders. Attendees commented that they never thought they'd see such a gathering beneath one roof, and they loved it. In 2013 the same event had sessions led by teams made up of pastors, intercessors, and worship leaders. For 2014, the plan is to focus the event as a workshop, mixing pastors, prayer leaders, and worship leaders to seek an answer to how the different giftings can be brought together for a more unified thrust to further God's kingdom and a clearer picture of how to make His house a house of prayer.

The Presence of the Father—the Worship Leaders' Perspective

Austin was made for worship. It's defined by its music—known as the Live Music Capital of the World. Every spring, thousands of people flock into Austin from all over the world to participate in the South by Southwest (SXSW) music and film festival. The SXSW website gives the history of the event[5], but as always, God has a bigger perspective. The story of God's work in this city would not be complete without a look at how He's dealt with the music scene here.

To get an inkling of where God has been in the Austin music scene, we need to start in the sixties. That decade shook with revolution and a quest for freedom. Martin Luther King led Black America in its march for equality and identity. The feminist movement called for women to stand up and be counted. Youth rejected their parents' values and formed the Hippy Movement. The status quo was shaken to the roots. The culture of the nation became a large chessboard where the devil used pride, hate, and rebellion as his players. In California, the Lord planted a man of love and righteousness, Holy Hubert Lindsey, to ignite the fire of the Jesus Movement. Young men and women from the hippy culture, who had stripped off the control and religious trappings of their time, came to know Jesus in a fresh, real way. One of the major changes they brought was in the beauty and simplicity of their worship—a new sound for a new day.

In Austin, a couple of early live music venues influenced the city and the nation. The Vulcan Gas Company portrayed a vivid picture of the hippy culture. Dick Pickens was working with the Teen Challenge Ministry right next door to the Vulcan. He tells his story:

> I had been a devoted fan of music from the blues of the 30s to the early rock of Buddy Holly. No music had really disturbed me until some of the sound of the mid-sixties. I did not think about it having spiritual impact until about 1968. I was no longer a radio deejay, and I realized I had become a bit insulated from the emerging scene of drugs, young crime, and its music. I quickly saw that my growing distaste with much of the current music had spiritual implications.
>
> When the then director of Austin's Teen Challenge, Rev. Royce Nimmons, suggested we go next door to the Vulcan Gas Company, I was not prepared for

what I saw and heard. The psychedelia, the driving sounds, and the behavior of the participants gave the impression of hell's likely frenzy. In fact, we literally felt sternum pressure that was akin to a heart attack. That's how strong it was sound-wise and spiritually.

After we left, we prayed, and we asked our prayer group to pray for clarity in how to deal with this. That is where we got the idea to give them God's music as an alternative—the music of the Jesus Movement. It was often up-tempo and fun, but did not have that demonic driving sound. That happened at The Well on 26th St. right off The Drag.[6]

The Vulcan closed in the summer of 1970. In August its replacement, the Armadillo World Headquarters, opened in the old National Guard Armory. It became the focus of a musical renaissance that made Austin a nationally recognized music capital.[7] The 'Dillo, as it was sometimes called, still reflected the negatives of the hippy culture, but it also had some interesting positives. It gave a place for young artists to have freedom of expression. They could explore new ways of thinking and new forms of both music and art.

June Criner, long-time intercessor for the city, expressed it this way. "It was free-flowing and a place to air your full creativity, which is what I believe God wants to do for the arts here." Along with the music, the poster art that went along with the 'Dillo helped open the door to freedom of expression in the arts. Where there is freedom, there are also excesses, but the space to develop a brand of creativity never seen before made the atmosphere of Austin pregnant with possibility.

Genesis 50:20 But as for you, you meant evil against me;
but God meant it for good, in order to bring it about as it is this
day, to save many people alive.

The enemy meant the rebellion of the sixties for destruction, and truly there has been much destruction, but God meant it for good, to tear down the social and religious structures that keep the creative spirit in bondage. Gregg Barnes, head of The Burn Austin, puts it this way:

> The problem is the church has been watching the world and trying to imitate the world. The world has led the way for the past couple of hundred years. If you go back to Michelangelo, he set the standard. He was worshipping God with his art. We've seen the shift from the church being the lead to the church being the tail. It's about taking back what touches hearts. It's the creative that touches hearts. The most effective tool of evangelism is worship. It's art—music and art, all forms of art. Music acts as a transport agent. Music takes the sound and the words straight to the spirit. That's why there's such a battle for worship over Austin. We know the battle over Austin has always been worship. Music and arts are part of that. Anything we do creative is worship if we do it toward God.

With an atmosphere of freedom and creativity released in Austin, it was only a matter of time until God's people began to take hold of it. The Well was the first live worship to touch the city—then the lively music of March for Jesus. Graham Kendrick, an Englishman, wrote the first music for the March, but it touched the heart of Austin and broke forth from here across the nation and around the globe. Shortly thereafter, the young worship leader from Austin Stone, Chris Tomlin, began to release songs that changed worship in Austin and far beyond. Faron Dice, general manager of WAY-FM Satellite Network, said, "The Tomlin music says things we want to say from the depths of our being." In 1997 Tomlin teamed up with Louie Giglio to host the first Passion Conference in Austin. Passion is a spiritual awakening gathering that hosts tens of thousands of college students every year. The worship from these conferences finds its way into church services all over the world.

Chris Tomlin moved to Atlanta, but since that time, the Lord has been calling worship leaders to the Austin area in droves and with purpose. Gregg Barnes has lived in Austin and led worship for a long time. Since connecting with Sean Feucht and The Burn in 2007, Gregg has been organizing and leading Burns, twenty-four hour worship events, all over the area. Gregg has watched the Lord open doors for him in a big circle around the city, like the spokes of a large wagon wheel. He and his intercessor wife, Machelle, know that worship draws the presence of God. They've sensed the atmosphere shift in place after place as worship teams from many area churches man their shifts and enter into that presence.

After Pray 40 in 2011, Bethany Martin, a songwriter and worship leader, was invited to the gathering of intercessors that led to the birth of Austin Kingdom Intercessors. She didn't know why she was invited, but felt like she was supposed to go. During the meeting she felt God's call to connect worship across the city and also to unite the houses of prayer. She shared what she was hearing with the group who confirmed what she had heard in many ways. She and her husband, David, were given the Live Worship Capital™ domain, which they use to promote the worship movement in the city and to lift up young artists. They helped start the Heart of Texas House of Prayer (HOTHOP) in Leander. From June 19 to September 17, 2012, they hosted ninety days of 24/7 prayer and worship with ninety churches and ministries taking part.

The first event Live Worship Capital sponsored was to host Rick Pino in July 2011. During one of the services, Rick prophesied:

> I'm telling you this worship thing is going to explode like the world has never seen. I believe the eyes of the world will be on Austin, Texas, because God is going to make this city a place known far and wide . . . a place of his presence and his glory . . . a place where you, Lord, have established your

tent peg here in this region . . . a tent peg put down in this city, God. Continue to unite the churches. Continue to unite the leadership and the apostolic dudes and gals here in this city. Continue to unite the Houses of Prayer. Give us a spirit of unity and command a blessing on that, Lord! We ask in Jesus name.[8]

In March of 2012, Rick Pino and Sean Feucht came back to Austin to do a Fire on the Altar, fifty hours of non-stop praise and worship. Then Pino moved to Austin, along with many other musicians who love Jesus. Bethany Martin says, "People will be moving here because of worship and because of the glory of God, not because of people or ministry, but because of the glory."

God isn't finished writing the Austin story

Austin is the fastest growing large city in the nation. As of February 2014, people are moving to Austin at the rate of 110 per day.[9] (That number seems to increase weekly.) They come for the economy. They come for education. They come for the technology. They come for the freedom of expression. Some come because God told them to. They come to add their page to the story of Austin.

Moses Austin had a big vision, but never in his wildest dreams could he have imagined what has happened here. Only God could see how this venture would unfold, and He's not finished yet. He's promised true reformation for Austin.[10] It will happen, because our God is faithful. In actuality, it is already happening, and those who have gone before, those who are here now, and those who are yet to come all have their part to play. The Lord takes all of our gifts and all of our passions and blends them together for all of our benefit, that *we may grow up in all things into Him who is the head—Christ— from whom the whole body, joined and knit together by what every joint supplies, according to the effective working by which every part does its share, causes growth of the body for the edifying of itself in love.*

Questions to consider

1. First write the question: What does it take to transform a _____ (city, community, church, family—you fill the blank.) Think about it from as many perspectives as you can think of.
2. With what piece of transformation do you identify? Where do you fit personally and where does the group you associate with fit into the larger scheme of things?
3. How does your group compliment the whole?
4. What do you need from others, which is beyond your scope, for the transformation?
5. What individuals, groups or entities have the gifting and call to fill those places?
6. In what ways could you work together?

END NOTES

1. http://www.christtogethergreateraustin.com/
2. http://www.christtogethergreateraustin.com/acts-of-service/
3. http://www.christtogethergreateraustin.com/circles-of-accountability/
4. http://www.austinprays.org/
5. http://sxsw.com/about/sxsw-history, accessed January 31, 2014.
6. (See the story of The Well in Chapter 3.)
7. http://www.tshaonline.org/handbook/online/articles/xda01/, accessed January 31.
8. http://www.abbaconnect.net/fire-on-the-altar/, accessed January 31, 2014.
9. Colin Pope, "How many people move to Austin a day? Here's the official number," *Austin Business Journal*, Feb. 14, 2014.
10. See the prophetic word from June 20, 2002, in the prophecy section in the back of this book.

EPILOGUE

There is no end to God's story. We serve an eternal Lord who dwells in the eternal now. The people who walk through the pages of this book as history are all part of the great cloud of witnesses. They filled their spot in this realm called time, and now they cheer us on as we build upon what they accomplished. As we step into the synergy of the generations, we drink from the wells they dug; we draw from the lessons they learned; and we understand that what they deposited in the spirit realm is still there for us to draw on. Each day we stand at the juncture where past meets future, and we add our pieces and our perspectives to God's story. Our pieces will be there for our grandchildren to build on. I pray that what you have read here will inspire you to add your piece with renewed confidence of its value, and that you will have an ever-growing appreciation for the pieces of others, for God writes His story through the pages of our lives. It takes all of us.

Austin through the Ages

1730	The Spanish set up a mission near current Barton Springs. The mission was later moved to San Antonio.
1820	Moses Austin purchased land in Central Texas from the Mexican Government. His son, Stephen F. Austin, handpicked 300 men to settle the territory.
1835	Anglo-American settlers began arriving in the area.
1836	Texas won its independence from Mexico.
1837	Anglo-American settlers founded the village of Waterloo in 1837, along the banks of the Colorado River. After the republic purchased several hundred acres to establish the city, Mirabeau Lamar, President of the Republic of Texas, renamed it Austin in honor of Stephen F. Austin in March of 1839.
1839	Presbyterians held the first protestant church service.
1839	The city of Austin was chartered.
1840	On January 25, President Lamar approved the act passed by the 4th Congress, creating the County of Travis and naming Austin as the capital of Texas.

1845   The Texas Annexation of 1845 was the annexation of the Republic of Texas to the United States of America as the 28th state.

1847   Methodists dedicated the first permanent church building.

1847   R. H. Taliaferro organized the First Baptist Church in Austin.

1848   The first Episcopal Church was organized.

1854   Mayor Rip Ford and a group of vigilantes forced most of Austin's Hispanic residents to leave the city. They felt the presence of the Hispanics gave African-American slaves "false notions of freedom."

1861–65 The Civil War dominated life in Austin.

1864   Jacob Fountaine founded First Baptist Church (colored) after emancipation.

1866–58 Jim Crow laws were passed to counter the nation's desegregation laws.

1870   Ku Klux Klan was established.

1872   Austin was officially chosen as the capital of the state of Texas.

1881   Austin became the home of the University of Texas. Tillotson Collegiate and Normal Institute was founded.

**1894
–1950**   African American revival meetings were held every August on the "Old Saint John Encampment Grounds," the current sight of Highland Mall.

1902   In the Liberty Hill area a revival began which was referred to as "Loafer's Glory." It lasted around twenty years.

1928   A city plan, which recommended that East Austin be designated a Negro district, was put in place. Municipal services, like schools, sewers and parks, were made available to blacks in East Austin only. Waller Creek and then I-35 have been dividing lines in the city.

1940   Austin's Hispanic residents, who in 1900 composed just 1.5 % of the population, rose to 11% by 1940.

1942   Central Assembly of God was birthed from healing services.

1948   Emma Long was elected as the first woman to the City Council.

1950   *Sweatt v. Painter* required the University of Texas Law School to admit African-American students, thereby breaking with segregation in the South's graduate and professional schools.

1952   Houston and Tillotson Colleges merge to form Houston-Tillotson College.

1954–84 Nuns, located in Tarrytown, prayed 24/7 for Austin for thirty   years.

1956   The University of Texas admitted African American students.

1964   Father Richard McCabe, a Roman Catholic priest, founded Caritas to help connect people experiencing poverty and homelessness with public assistance.

1970   Crop Hunger Walk raised money to aid the poor.

1970   The Armadillo Headquarters opened, paving the way for Austin to become the live music capital of the world.

1970   The Well, under the Teen Challenge ministry, was the first venue for live Christian music.

1976   A citywide campaign called "Here's Life, Austin," under the headship of Campus Crusade, sponsored the "I Found it" campaign.

1977   Dan Davis founded Hope Chapel and began building relationships with other pastors in the city. Those relationships became the foundation for much of the unity that followed.

1978   The first South by Southwest (SXSW) Music festival was held.

1988   The American Atheists Association opened their general headquarters in Austin.

1988   At about the same time Madelyn O'Hare was founding the Atheist Association, God spoke through June Criner to declare that He had chosen Austin and that His children, by His Spirit, would rise up and take this land.

1988–89 A prayer group from Hope Chapel did spiritual mapping in Austin.

1989   Tom Pelton brought the March for Jesus to Austin.

1990   The first "Praise March" took place Austin.

1991   The March for Jesus US was launched from the city.

1991   God gave Jeremy Story, then a student of the University of Texas, the vision for Campus Renewal Ministries.

1993   Ed Silvoso prophesied that Austin would be one of four first cities to have transformation in the United States.

1996   More than sixty-five pastors signed a covenant for racial reconciliation.

1996–97 Citywide prayer events took place, involving a mixed leadership of Hispanic and Anglo pastors and intercessors.

1997   More than twenty campus ministers met together to discuss what it meant to work together for transformation at UT.

1998   Pastors in Covenant (PIC) was established to give pastors small group fellowship and support with other pastors.

1998   June Criner called a 24/7 Solemn Assembly for seven days straight with other citywide intercessors, worshipping, fasting, and praying for transformation.

1999   The American Atheist Association moved their headquarters to New Jersey.

1999   On New Year's Eve, to bring in the new millennium, over 5,000 Christians united at the Frank Erwin Center to celebrate Jesus. Over 252 churches were represented at the event. It was the first Christian event ever held at the Frank Erwin Center.

2000   Austin to Jesus (A2J) hosted forty hours of united, continual prayer over the turn of the millennium (Dec. 31 – January 1).

2000   Citywide Prayer launched in January 2000, led by Daniel Geraci, continued for the next fourteen months, gathering over 3,000 Christians to unite in prayer for city transformation.

2000   Austin's first citywide Christian calendar, AustinforJesus.com, was launched to enable Christians to post citywide events, concerts, outreaches, etc

2000   The Commitment to Racial Reconciliation made important strides towards reconciliation.

2001   Texas Jesus Video Project mailed 2,600,000 videos throughout the state.

2001   Sheep Pen 78723 brought together pastors (especially Hispanic pastors) and intercessors to prayer walk and stake zip codes 78723 and 78752. Crime rates dropped, and some undesirable businesses left the area as a result.

2002   The first 24/7 house of prayer was held on the UT campus during REZ Week

2002   Austin Bridge Builders Alliance (ABBA) was founded.

2002   Benjamin Anyacho launched citywide prophetic prayer meetings.

2002   Reconciliation occurred between pastors and intercessors when Ed Silvoso came to Austin with "Anointed for Business" and "City Reaching" meetings.

2002–06 Vicky Porterfield headed Pray Austin, a multi-denominational team created to build prayer as an essential tool of revival in the Austin area.

2003   Austin Latin Ministerial Alliance (ALMA), an alliance of Hispanic pastors, was formed.

2003   Pastors' Prayer Gatherings became a vital part of the Pastors in Covenant movement. Pastors had been meeting yearly for prayer summits for some years.

2003–08 Luke 4:18 raises up 24/7 prayer – Seek God for the City.

2004–08 City Impact Roundtable meetings were held in conjunction with Mission America .

2004   The tsunami in Indonesia drew a united effort of assistance from churches in Austin. It made them see the need for greater unity and preparations to address possible future disasters in our area.

2005   Hurricane Katrina sent thousands of homeless people to Austin. The church in Austin gathered around ABBA's leadership to meet the need. It helped define ABBA's place as a credible connector for the city.

2005   Lori DeVillez opened the first Austin Pregnancy Resource Center, and soon formed the Austin Area Life Affirming Coalition to unite life-affirming groups.

2005–10 Events were organized to celebrate the Global Day of Prayer. Most years they included ten days of 24/7 prayer at Austin House of Prayer (AHOP) leading up to Pentecost.

2005   Sacred Trust and Watchmen groups brought intercessors together.

2005   Austin House of Prayer (AHOP) opened.

2006   The first Hope Fest, a church-based family day at Regan High School, united city agencies, schools, non-profits and churches working together to serve the needs of the community.

2006   Two Global Day of Prayer services were held at the Delco Center – one English, one Spanish. The Spanish service included Catholic participation and identificational repentance from white leaders for the treatment of Hispanics in our city.

2007   Local pastors invited Francis Frangipane to speak at Burger Center. Around 700 attended. This event provided significant impact for unity.

2008   Pastor Trey Kent started the Unceasing Prayer Movement with churches joining forces to pray 24/7 for the city.

2008   Gregg and Machelle Barnes started Burn Austin, bringing churches together for twenty-four hours of continuous worship in many areas of Greater Austin.

2008–09 The "In the City for the City" events at the Bob Bullock Museum drew churches, ministries, non-profits, and government agencies together to see that joining resources multiplies everyone's effectiveness in the city.

2009   The Pastors' Strategic Council was formed.

2009   Daniel Geraci founded the Austin Disaster Relief Network (ADRN)

2010   Greater Impact for Greater Austin – more than 200 pastors gathered to hear about a survey that showed how the church was impacting the city and to consider the Pastors' Strategic Council's plea for unity. Pastors' Strategic Council adopts "In the City for the City" as a promotional theme.

2010   Austin Stone hosted the first Verge Conference, promoting missional communities.

2010   The International House of Prayer in Kansas City prophesied revival in Austin.

2011   Pray Forty—forty days of prayer and worship led up to Lent.

2011   Walls Campaign—churches all over the area did the same sermon series and sponsored small group with the purpose of breaking down the barriers in our lives and in the city.

2011   Austin Disaster Relief Network led area efforts to deal with a flood in Williamson County and fires in Oak Hill, Leander, and Bastrop.

2012   Rick Pino and Sean Feucht organized a fifty-hour non-stop praise and worship event called "Fire on the Altar." Large numbers of worship leaders began moving into the area.

2013   Pastors invited atheist leaders to a friendly discussion. An abortion bill brought thousands of demonstrators to the Texas State Capitol. The Explore God Campaign involved 377 churches in an effort to engage the city in spiritual conversations.

PROPHETIC WORDS OVER GREATER AUSTIN

From the Author

I realize this is only a sampling of prophetic words spoken over Austin. Some are well known and were given by recognized prophetic voices. Some came from individuals in prayer meetings or church services. I know there are many more prophecies concerning Central Texas. If you know of any I don't have, I would love to have you send it/them to me at thana@abbaconnect.net. I will continue to collect the words God has spoken through His people over this area.

What God Has Said about Austin

1988   June Criner: "So do you believe I can change the face of a city? Is my power great enough? Yea, I tell you I can move any mountain. I have chosen this place as I have chosen Zion, and I will dwell in it, and many will come and say, 'Let's go to Austin. You can see God there. He lives there. You can be healed there, because God lives there. You can rejoice and praise there, because God lives there.' I will touch all areas of this city. None will be untouched. My children will rise up by My Spirit and by My Wisdom and take this land that is close to My heart. I will sweep away all hindrances, not because of anyone, but because of My Name, and I choose to show Myself strong. Stand at attention. Wait for the battle cry and then proceed. It will be beyond your wildest imaginings. Multitudes of souls will cry out unto My Name from one end of this city to the other, 'JESUS IS LORD!'"

1994   Ed Silvoso prophesied that Austin would be one five cities where revival will start for the nation.

1995   Barbara Wentroble: "As the days of Noah and the waters cover the earth, so will be glory of God cover the region."

1998   June Criner, along with some intercessors and worship leaders, called the solemn assembly because they felt like the Lord was saying that 24/7 praise and prayer would set the enemies of the city to flight. (A few months later the American Atheist Association moved its headquarters out of Austin.)

June 20, 2002 Chuck Pierce: "I gave a word on December the 8th concerning Austin. I just reread that word. What it said was that something was going on in this city and if you would start having prayer meetings once a month for eight months you would start seeing some change in the city. This city was once prophesied in Argentina (many of you know that I have been in and out of Argentina since the early 90's) it was prophesied this would be the first city of true transformation in our nation. And that came from some of the Argentines. And yet every time this city starts moving forward, it's as if scattering occurs and there's a stop put on it. I want to tell you it could be that God is saying right now it is time for this city to move forward and that this city itself will be a sign to our nation one way or the other. Now, what I want us to understand is the light's about to get lighter and the dark's about to get darker."

The prophecy: "And the spirit of God said, 'I am sending a sign of hail upon this state.' Now hear me, now write this down, because we're people that don't understand signs, and we don't know how to move in signs. And He said, 'I'm going to start sending a sign of hail on this state in the next two months. When you see hail fall in your city, know that it is time for the heavens and the atmosphere to change. At that time, declare where hell on earth has controlled your city—declare to hell that the hail from heaven is a change that it is losing, is a sign that (hell) is about to lose it's authority in your city. Declare it is a time for change and that everything hell is holding captive in your city, the resources both physical as well as material that have been held back and robbed from the church, declare that both will start being let go. This is a key time. I am changing the atmosphere of heaven even now over this state. Watch for the changing and watch for the signs and move accordingly' saith the Lord."

(July 1, 2002 from Bob Long: "I have received numerous reports from all over Austin regarding prayer ministries and their response as it hailed this past Wednesday night in Austin. Tonight (Monday) I am receiving emails from intercessors in El Paso that El Paso received hail last night. They used the prophetic words from Chuck as strategy and declaration for the entire city.")

2005   Daniel Geraci received the vision for ADRN. It came to pass in 2009.

2005   Samuel Brassfield gave a prophecy about I 35 being a Highway of Holiness

2006   In the midst of a message at a "Start the Year Out Right" conference in Denton, Texas, where Dutch Sheets was sharing things God had shown him, he said there was going to be a move of God on the UT campus.

2006 From Lance Bane, youth pastor at Church of the Hills: "Then to my surprise, a high school girl from COTH (Church of the Hills) walked up to me, innocently and confidently. She said, 'Pastor Lance, I want to share with you what God was speaking to me during our prayer time tonight.' Of course, I wanted to hear this, and she shared with me this clear word for our city:

1. "The spiritual winds are changing and the Lord is stirring up something new and big in Austin. But there are things polluting the pureness of His winds—counterfeit.

2. "God is calling Austin the 'Prodigal Son.' We will be the first of the returning cities to the Father. Jeremiah 3:14–15, 'Return, o faithless sons (other cities, states, nations),' declares the Lord. 'For I am a master to you . . . and I will bring you to Zion, then I will give you shepherds after my own heart (Austinites) who will feed you on knowledge and understanding. Austin will set the example, and soon after, many cities, states, and nations will follow in our footsteps.

3. "Jeremiah 3.19 'How I would set you among my sons, and give you a pleasant land, the most beautiful inheritance of the nations. And I said you shall call me Father and not turn away from following me.' The favor of the Lord will rest upon Austin, and He will call the city 'the most beautiful inheritance of the nations.'"

February 20, 2009 Ras Robinson: "The Lord says, 'A convergence of revival and transformation is about to spring up in Austin. This city is on My map for the future of the Kingdom of God. I will touch every aspect of life in Austin. Intercession and prayers will burst forth in unison. Yes, I say unto you, I will use three things in this sovereign move, unified prayer and intercession, unified concerts of praise and worship, and unified prophetic expounding of My word in every nook and cranny of Austin.

'You have done well to identify the prophetic seven mountains of Austin. And yes, I am causing an eighth mountain to suddenly appear which will be called the mountain of God even Sinai. From this place I will speak governments and My order in these last days.

'By faith, even that of a mustard seed, you will cast the present mountains of wickedness, debauchery, pride in being weird as to mock Me into the sea. This will proceed simultaneously with the emerging of My mountain.

'

Much as has happened in Wales, Fiji, Guatemala, Columbia and many other places, there will be a springing forth of revival and transformation, not engineered by man, but through a divine visitation of My Spirit, says the Lord. Can you imagine My goodness to do this. I say unto you, taste and see that the Lord is good, blessed is the one who takes refuge in me.

'Now, find your faith as a mustard seed and let us begin.'"

January 21, 2010 Art Serna of Rally Call at City Prayer:
Art Serna had a powerful word. He saw two angels, one called Might and the other Abundance. He prophesied, "Look to the south because the hemisphere below will be brought to this city. Build the infrastructure that will sustain millions who will come from the nations. Do you have the infrastructure to withstand what will come to you?"

Art felt God was saying millions would come. Build an infrastructure. Prepare for it. It's going to come. He prayed we would create the infrastructure of communication and resources. Prophetically he continued, "The finger of God is on venture capitalists in this region. I'm going to touch them in a way that they're going to create the wineskins that will hold revival and awakening in the land and in the nations. The Lord says, 'I'm going to put my finger upon them. They are going to think in a different way.' The Lord says, 'I am going to raise them from this very region. They will come from this place. They will have new paradigms to think nation building – the ability to multiply – and that word that has gone forth about eradicating systemic poverty.' the Lord says Austin has the ability and the spirit to implement something that is practical, sustainable, and lasting to touch that in the nations of the earth and to bring change."

January 21, 2010 (same meeting as last word) Lawrence Babin of Church of the Hills: "Seymour couldn't stay in Houston because of a religious spirit. A religious spirit also ended the Azusa Street revival. I had a dream about old ruins and God's presence was ordering everything. We've been experiencing broken hearts in a way I can't really put words to. Everyone that begins to walk in His love – that which you touch is going to receive mercy. Mercy triumphs over judgment, so what we deserve, we don't actually get. When a city taps into the heart of God, we can't comprehend the power. The Great Awakening was when everybody came into a realization of the love of God. Hearts change. God changes the hearts, but we must demonstrate His love, so I carry the authority of love. If I demonstrate that on the street, they see Christ."

February 2010 During a time of outpouring at the International House of Prayer in Kansas City, one of the leaders turned to the camera and said, "Austin, Texas, you're next."

February 11, 2010 From City Prayer

"And I say to you I am blessed, and I am smiling as this occurs. And I will pour forth My Spirit upon central Texas. And I will break down the strongholds because of the worship and the unity that I see in my people that is coming together by My Spirit and by your obedience. Continue this. Be unified; be in prayer. Pray it in and it shall be."

Same meeting, Bruce Cook of K.E.Y.S. (Kingdom Economic Yearly Summit): "Where Austin has been an importer of things of the spirit, the Lord says, 'I'm bringing equilibrium to the city, and it shall become an exporter.' The Lord says, 'Austin is a prototype city, because I'm raising up nameless, faceless people to lead movements and to lead ministries, even as the fire is already going out through Campus Renewal. It's already going out through K.E.Y.S. It's already going out to other places through a number of ministries in the Austin area."

July 2, 2011 Rick Pino's word released at River of the Hills: "When we try and we strive . . . just feel the love of God. Dude, just let it go man. Just realize that your Father loves you and He's crazy about you and you can't do anything, so just give up into His arms and see where He takes you. He wants to give you a voice that would so shake this city. I'm telling you this worship thing is going to explode like the world has never seen. I believe the eyes of the whole world will be on Austin, Texas, because God is going to make this city a place known far and wide. This city is a place of His presence and His glory."

August 6, 2011 Summation of a word given by Bob Jones at the Kingdom Ministries Conference at Cathedral of Praise: "There are two gardens—Eden and Gethsemane. We have been looking to return to Eden. Jesus is calling us to Gethsemane. This is the place of death to self and where Jesus took up the mantle of his Father's will.

"It is August in Austin. The word of the Lord will be exalted here. Death to self is the beginning of the walking in the spirit, and it must happen here. Focus on the restoration of all things rather than revival. This is the 3rd wave that is coming. It is waist high. Not like the 4th wave that is yet to come without measure. God has you when you are committed from the waist down. He wants commitment. From the waist up- we will have a nurturing nature for the souls to be saved. There will be healing and words of knowledge released like never before. Those who are faithful will receive. Out of the great cloud of witnesses in Hebrews 12, will come revelations, as these witnesses are investors in us. Revelation will be given; the purpose of heaven will be given for the will of God in your life. Continual signs and wonders will flow.

"Intercessors—all of HEAVEN is behind you! The church is at the bottom of the pit and the leaders have to come up and be cleansed. Go to the garden to die to self. Selfishness no longer has a place. All churches belong to GOD!"

March 4, 2012 Sam Brassfield for Round Rock at Fire on the Altar: (Concerning the rock in the river for which Round Rock is named) "I heard the Lord say, 'That stone there, I am going to Round Rock, Texas. I am drawing a fifty-mile radius around Round Rock. And I'm calling it Bethel, the House of God.' And He said, 'Jollyville will be jolly once again.' There is something happening in Jollyville that the Lord likes, and He is bringing joy back to Jollyville once again. And this is what He said. I didn't question the Lord . . . I just kept sitting there and just soaking and soaking and in the back of my mind I said, 'Why did you choose Round Rock? Why did you say Round

Rock?' And I didn't ask the Lord, I was just wondering in my mind, and he came over to me and said, 'You know what happened there son? A long time ago, a group of people came there, and there was a pastor that came there to the creek. They were baptizing people there, and he got up on that round rock, and he declared and he said, "Lord, would you bring revival there to Austin?" He was there! So let there be a fifty-mile radius around Round Rock where the glory of the Lord will be shown! This was a place where I met with a man, and I made a promise, and I will keep my promise.' So there are waves of glory. Now, don't go there and make a monument. This is just an area that has been established as the House of God. There will be signs and wonders and miracles. Revival is breaking out! . . . He said, 'There are wells here all over this area that I am digging. The artesian waters, coming straight from the throne room, are starting to bubble up all over!'"

June 29, 2013 Cindy Jacobs prophecy over Austin at the Tabernacle of David Conference at PromiseLand:
"You will rebuild the Tabernacle of David, and I am going to begin to inhabit the praises of My people. The Lord says, 'Look and I will do a new thing. It looks like great darkness and a day of gloom, but I say arise and shine, for your light is come.' For I see rain to bring a new Jesus People movement. You have circuit riders and a pioneer anointing. The Lord showed me there are mantels going to be poured out. There's going to be a mantel for circuit riders."

INDEX

CPSIA information can be obtained at www.ICGtesting.com
Printed in the USA
LVOW12s2354050514

384502LV00002B/2/P